philippians

A 90-Day Devotional
on the Book of Philippians

By Dr. Deborah Waterbury

First Printing by Love Everlasting Ministries in 2016

Second Printing by DebWaterbury, Inc. 4/21/2017

ISBN-13: 978-0998920863

ISBN-10: 099892086X

BISAC: Religion / Biblical Studies / Paul's Letters

Library of Congress Control Number: 2017905976

Printed in the United States of America

Introduction

One of the most rewarding ways to study the bible is expositionally. Whereas reading through God's Word for content and personal meaning has great impact within the life of the believer, breaking the verses apart and digging deeper for context and language will bring enlightenment beyond simple reading.

Additionally, daily devotional time is paramount for every Christian. All of us need some amount of time with our Father every day, and daily devotion guides are an excellent tool in this endeavor. There are so many wonderful devotionals on the market today that none of us has an excuse for not having that personal time every day.

It is with these two thoughts in mind that I developed my series for daily devotionals. Each book, in this case the book of Philippians, is broken up into a short expositional devotion taken verse by verse so that the reader is actually doing a complete study of the book while she spends needed time with her Father each day. Each devotion is designed so that it can be completed in fifteen minutes or less with everything the reader needs right here in this book to have her daily personal time.

Each day begins with the verse(s) consecutively written out, followed by a short exposition and application. Next the reader will have a "Study/Meditation" question for further contemplation, which is followed by a short optional prayer. Once the reader has completed this short daily devotion guide, she will have done a complete expositional study of the book.

It will always be my contention that our lives are fully incomplete as believers unless we know our Father and Savior better. What better way is there to do that than to study His Holy Word more indepth? I realize that many of the reasons some of us have for not having a personal quiet time with God is no time and no idea of what to do. These devotions are short, complete, and allow deep study without a lot of preparation or too much time.

I pray that since you've picked this book up long enough to read the Introduction that you will also dedicate that fifteen minutes each day to your Lord. I promise you that only peace and joy come from spending time with Him. I promise you that He is there. I promise you that it will not be time ill spent, and I promise you that study of God's Word will only bring deeper communion with Him and exceedingly more understanding of who He is.

God bless you.

Are You a Slave?

It was traditional in antiquity for the writer of a letter to introduce himself in the very first few words. Whereas Timothy was not writing this letter with Paul since Paul refers to himself in the letter in first person and refers to Timothy in the third person, Timothy was most likely there with Paul, serving as a secretary of sorts. Paul then introduces them both to his Philippian audience, and the way he does so teaches us much about how we are to view ourselves in relation to Christ.

Paul uses the word "servant" or "slave" to describe both himself and Timothy. Literally the word was "bond servant," which was used to illustrate ones obligatory, subordinate role under the authority of another. Paul unabashedly calls himself a slave to Christ, and even though the connotation of that word often offends, the truth is that we are all slaves to something. Paul wrote in Romans 6:16, "Do you not know that if you present yourselves to anyone as obedient slaves, you are slaves of the one who you obey, either of sin, which leads to death, or of obedience, which leads to righteousness?"

The question we must ask ourselves is, "To whom am I a slave?" Many people call themselves Christians, but day in and day out they are only slaves to themselves. There is only one Lord and that is not self. So as we begin this study of Philippians together, let us ask ourselves if we are happily enslaved to Christ, our Savior and Bridegroom. Paul was, and he readily identified himself in such a manner.

(continued)

– Study/Meditation –

Read Romans 6:15-23.
How does Paul describe being a "slave to righteousness"?

Father, I am your slave, and I am so privileged to be so.
Thank You for Your abounding mercy and love in
bringing me into Your kingdom. Amen.

Christians as Saints

Philippians 1:1b

"To all the saints in Christ Jesus who are at Philippi, with the overseers and deacons."

You may read a greeting like this from the Apostle Paul to the Philippian church and think he was greeting some special select group there, some "super Christians" who had done a great work or a glorious service so that they had received the title of "saint." Unfortunately, the word "saint" has often been misused; it was biblical in its usage when referring to all true Christians. In fact, Paul had written to the saints in Philippi, Ephesus, Rome, and even Corinth as he wrote to the entire church.

The word "saint" simply means "holy one." To be holy means to be "set apart." Christians are those who have been set apart for Christ. Believers have been set apart for Christ in that they have accepted His sacrifice and His lordship so that God has forgiven them of their sins. They have been therefore "set apart" from this evil world, set apart from serving themselves and their sinful natures, and instead set apart in Christ to do His will. Paul was greeting all of those who had been set apart by God in Christ to do His will and to live to His glory.

Christians, or saints, are to live in the world but to live as one who is set apart from it. That doesn't mean that they are to remove themselves from the world as in a monastery or somewhere else away from the rest of "ordinary people." On the contrary, they are to be in it to testify to Christ's saving work while they are obviously set apart as His. All believers, therefore, are saints, or holy ones set apart in Christ.

(continued)

Christians as Saints – continued

– Study/Meditation –

How are you to live day by day as one "set apart" for Christ?
What does that look like practically?

Father, help me in my endeavors to live in this world while set apart from it. Forgive me for the times when I fail and give me strength and wisdom to live correctly for You. Amen.

Peace in Grace

Philippians 1:2

*"Grace to you and peace from God our Father
and the Lord Jesus Christ."*

This greeting, which appeared in some form using "grace" and "peace" in all thirteen of Paul's letters, was a combination of traditional salutations in the Jewish and Greek societies. Paul begins this letter to the church in Philippi with the clear intention of not only introducing himself and providing the appropriate greeting, but with uniting them as Christians who have available to them grace and peace that only comes from God through Christ.

Grace is that gift one receives due to unmerited favor. If you think you've done something to earn favor or reward, then you do not receive grace. Grace is given to us by God due to His own character and of His own will. We deserve His wrath. He chooses to give us His grace. If for some reason you think that you can gain God's favor by being good enough or living cleanly enough, then you do not yet know God's grace. Only by seeing how undeserving we are of eternity can we be the recipients of this gift. Peace, on the other hand, is the result of receiving God's grace.

True peace comes when a person knows that God's grace has been bestowed upon him, and he thereby can live in contentment now with God, with himself, and with others. Grace and peace begin vertically, but will always extend horizontally. Those of us who know God's grace and have peace with Him because of it will naturally seek to both show grace to others and live peaceably with them.

(continued)

Peace in Grace – *continued*

– Study/Meditation –

Read Romans 4:1-8. How does Paul connect faith and grace?

Father, thank You for giving me Your grace so that I can experience peace with You and with others. Help me to extend grace to others as I have had it shown to me. Amen.

Joy in Prayer

Philippians 1:3-4

"I thank my God in all my remembrance of you, always in every prayer of mine for you all making my prayer with joy."

Paul knew the secret to attaining true joy, and it is founded in the Holy Spirit and through the outpouring of relationship. Don't misidentify joy for happiness. Being happy is a response to circumstance. Joy is the result of right relationship. Paul was sitting in prison upon writing this letter to the Philippian church. It's a pretty sure bet that he wasn't exceedingly happy in his circumstances. However, he knew how to seek joy, and that was in remembering his brothers and sisters in Christ and praying for them.

The ability to do this sort of remembering and focused prayer can only come from a joy that first originates with a right relationship with God. When we have peace with Him, being assured of our salvation and eternity with Him, then joy permeates our situations in life and naturally pours forth in joy toward those who share this experience with us. As a matter of fact, we know that trials and persecution don't touch joy if it's the joy of the Spirit in a Spirit-filled life. On the contrary, these circumstances may become occasions of deeper joy because they cast the believer totally off his circumstances and on to his God. It's in that relationship, its depth, that real joy is found.

Are you looking for true joy today? If so, look no further than to your relationship with your Father and then remember and pray for your fellow brothers and sisters. Your circumstances, no matter how dire, will not permeate your state of heart in this eternal perspective.

(continued)

– Study/Meditation –

Think of at least two fellow Christians you can pray for today and lift them up in prayer. Why do you think this is a path to the joy we all have in Christ?

Father, my hope and my joy is in You. I love You and I give You all the praise and glory and honor in my life. Amen.

The Church Family

Philippians 1:5

*"...because of your partnership in the gospel
from the first day until now."*

The following analogy was given some years ago: A family went to the movies together. They went in and sat down, but the youngest of the sons stayed in the lobby to get some popcorn. When he finally got through the long line at the concession stand with his refreshments, the movie had already begun. He stood at the back of the dark, crowded theater, looking unsuccessfully for his family. Finally from the back of the auditorium he yelled, "Does anyone in here know me? Does anyone recognize me?"

Unfortunately, that is how many people feel when they enter their local churches. It is supposed to be filled with their brothers and sisters in Christ, but when push comes to shove, they don't feel like anyone in the crowded room even knows them. That is not the way it should be when we meet together as a church family, and it is not the way it was in Philippi. Paul began his letter by telling this church that he thanked God every day for them, for their partnership with him in ministry. He remembered them in love because they were his family and they made sure he knew it.

When you walk into your church, do you ever feel like that little boy in the movie theater, searching desperately for someone who might know you? Or are you one of the members who are content to sit in the pews, looking straight ahead, making no effort to either greet your family or be greeted by them? Our church is our family, our God-centered family. Let us strive to greet one another as such, making sure every member of the family knows that they are known.

(continued)

5

The Church Family – *continued*

– Study/Meditation –

What active plan do you have to make your church
more like your family in Christ?

*Father, thank You for giving me brothers and sisters in You. Help me to both seek
them out as well as avail myself to them as they seek me out. Amen.*

He Will Complete It

Philippians 1:6

*"And I am sure of this, that he who began a good work in you will
bring it to completion at the day of Jesus Christ."*

Often we go through life feeling pretty much like we are failing at this "Christian thing." We say the wrong things, do the wrong things, make wrong decisions, and then feel like a complete failure at the end of the day. We feel many times like Paul in Romans 7:15 and 18 when he wrote, "I do not understand my own actions. For I do not do what I want, but I do the very thing I hate. For I know that nothing good dwells in me, that is, in my flesh. For I have the desire to do what is right, but not the ability to carry it out."

Paul was encouraging the Philippian church in their own sanctification so they would not lose heart, and he does so for you and me as well. It is God who is at work in us, even though we see in our body "another war waging war against the law of my mind," making us "captive to the law of sin." (Romans 7:23) We must remember that once we gave ourselves to our Father, accepting the salvation only available through His Son, the work began. It will not be finished until the day we stand in glory before Him, but it is happening. Remember that Paul also wrote a few verses later in Romans 8, "There is therefore now no condemnation for those who are in Christ Jesus."

Be encouraged, Christian. God will finish what He began in you, and it will come to completion. It is a work that only He can do, and He will do it! Amen!

(continued)

6

He Will Complete It – continued

– Study/Meditation –

What besetting sin plagues you most in your day-to-day life?
How can you preach truth to yourself to be encouraged, even as you
struggle in your flesh while on this earth? (Hint: Read Romans 8)

*Father, thank You for choosing me and for working in me,
even though I often don't see it. Give me the strength to persevere
in You as I work out my own salvation. Amen.*

How We View Church

Philippians 1:7

*"It is right for me to feel this way about you all, because I hold
you in my heart, for you are all partakers with me of grace,
both in my imprisonment and in the defense and
confirmation of the gospel."*

It is fully unfortunate that consumerism has permeated our idea of church today. The notion that church is the place where you go one or two times a week to have your needs met and then go home to your regular life would have been completely foreign to the Philippian church and to Paul. Often today we "church shop," going from church to church looking for the "right" one that satisfies our personal criteria for church. Then we take our seats in the pew and receive for an hour and half at which point we go home to our lives. Nervous pastors fret when members leave to go down the street to another church that seems to offer full service programs, so they get busy revamping their own services to further meet the public needs.

Church is not a place we go to be entertained or to have our needs met or to reflect mainstream society in whatever fashion is prevalent that day. Church is where we go in fellowship with other believers to worship and serve our risen Lord who bought us with His blood. Sometimes, as Paul indicated in his letter, that includes being persecuted. Paul tells the Philippian church that he remembers them with joy because they were partakers with him in both the grace they received from God but also in persecution.

Let us not be infiltrated by the world's idea of church, but instead be consumed with passion of like-minded believers who long for nothing else but communion based on Christ, a communion that shares in both the joy and the hardship.

(continued)

How We View Church – continued

– Study/Meditation –

How do you see church services in contemporary society often
straying from what Paul would consider correct church focus?
What attitudes in yourself need to be altered when you attend church
so that you are there for the right reasons?

*Father, thank You for giving me my local church. Help me attend as
a worshipper of You and of the Lord Jesus Christ, not for my own needs
to be met. Forgive me when I attend selfishly. Amen.*

Love One Another

Philippians 1:8

*"For God is my witness, how I yearn for you all
with the affection of Christ Jesus."*

There is no argument that just because we are brothers and sisters in Christ that loving each other can sometimes be difficult. Yet Paul uses the word "yearn" to describe how desperately he misses his Philippian church family. The Greek usage of this word was used to speak of one's intestines or inward parts. In other words, Paul was saying that his longing to be with them came from the deepest part of him.

Do we have that kind of longing to see our church family when we are away from them? The truth is that we should. Surely not everyone in the Philippian church was easy to get along with, so how could Paul yearn for their company so deeply? The key to this dilemma lies in the phrase "with the affection of Christ Jesus." Jesus cared for all of His children, regardless of their personality quirks, and He did so with such ferocity that He quite literally died for them.

We love each other through Christ. We look beyond our own sinful responses to the personalities and actions of our brothers and sisters toward the sin-erasing, wrath-removing love our Savior has for them. As we obey by seeking to eradicate our own judgmental, unloving reactions and instead move toward Christ's love for others, the feelings of love will naturally, and in time, follow.

(continued)

– Study/Meditation –

Think of at least one brother or sister in Christ that you have
a difficult time loving. What steps can you take so that you can grow
to love this person through the love Jesus already has for them?

*Father, forgive me for being unloving and judgmental of my brothers and sisters
at times. Help me as I endeavor to love with Your love. Amen.*

Biblical Love

Philippians 1:9

"And it is my prayer that your love may abound more and more, with knowledge and all discernment."

"Love" is often misused and misidentified within the Christian community. Some think that real love is devoid of intellect. They believe that we are to love by accepting the beliefs of anyone and everyone with no regard to the doctrinal authenticity of those beliefs. Love for these people is all heart and no head. Still others have gone to the opposite extreme, sacrificing kindness and patience in favor of strong doctrine. They feel love is intolerant to the extreme; it is all head and no heart. Paul realized that there is to be a fine balance between head and heart when it comes to biblical love, and it is in this kind of love that we are to "abound more and more."

Biblical love that is Christ exalting is in displaying kindness and self-sacrificial behavior toward others, but it is guided by "knowledge and all discernment." Knowledge that drives true love does not anchor itself in culture but in God. It is spiritual knowledge that finds its source in God's Word and in all Holy Spirit driven insight. True discernment comes only upon the foundation of Godly knowledge. One is discerning if he or she can correctly understand and identify truth as it is portrayed in the bible.

Consequently, Paul's prayer for the Philippian church, which should also be our prayer for ourselves and our brothers and sisters in Christ, is that we love one another with a Godly love, a love that is based on God's Word and that in that knowledge can identify the differences between good and evil. This is love that combines both heart and head in order to truly glorify our Lord.

(continued)

17

Biblical Love – continued

– Study/Meditation –

How can an incorrect balance between heart and
head cause damage within a church?

*Father, help me to love correctly with my head and my heart. Thank You for
giving me the Holy Spirit so that I might know these things. Amen.*

Loving in Excellence

Philippians 1:10

"(And it is my prayer that your love may abound more and more, with knowledge and all discernment), so that you may approve what is excellent, and so be pure and blameless for the day of Christ."

One of the biggest obstacles to purposeful Christian living is getting sidetracked onto things that aren't relevant, or as Paul calls them, "excellent." D. Martin Lloyd Jones said, ""The difficulty in life is to know on what we ought to concentrate. The whole art of life, I sometimes think, is the art of knowing what to leave out, what to ignore, what to put on one side. How prone we are to dissipate our energies and to waste our time by forgetting what is vital and giving ourselves to second and third rate issues" (The Life of Joy [Baker], p. 54). Paul's prayer for his brothers and sisters in the Philippian church was that they would cultivate and express Christ-like love toward each other that is centered on knowledge and discernment so that they would not be diverted onto worldly things of little or no importance.

It is our goal to apply a laser-like focus onto the things of God, recognizing the areas that both bring Him glory and show others His kingdom. When we do so, we live as "pure and blameless." This does not mean that we live as perfect and faultless, but as with integrity and right thoughts. It is interesting that Paul's focus for the Christian displaying these excellent and God-honoring qualities is in the way that we love one another. We do all of this with the understanding that Jesus is returning, a day when we will both be called home to Him and where we will be held to account for how our love abounded correctly for each other.

– Study/Meditation –

How does what Paul writes to the Philippian church in these verses much like what Jesus told His disciples in John 13:34-35?

Father, help me to see how I should love my brothers and sisters with excellence. Thank You for loving me this way. Amen.

Imputed Righteousness

Philippians 1:11

"...filled with the fruit of righteousness that comes through Jesus Christ, to the glory and praise of God."

What a beautiful thing that Paul prayed for his fellow Christians in this way! He prayed that they abound in a love for one another that is true and right so that they would be able to discern all that is excellent, and then he prayed for the sanctification that will surely take place in their lives because of Jesus.

We received the full measure of Christ's righteousness upon justification, but the fruit that is displayed because of that imputed righteousness is not instantaneous but a process. Paul's prayer, which should also be our desire, is that our lives are characterized by actions and deeds that exemplify our regenerated hearts, attributes which are only possible "through Jesus Christ." These deeds will certainly be manifested in discerning and correct love for one another, and our lives will be filled continually with the fruit that can only come from Christ's imputed righteousness.

Finally, all of these things are ultimately given so that our lives glorify the one, true living God, displaying His majesty to the entire world. In this we praise Him, and it is for this that Paul prays for us.

– Study/Meditation –

How can you display fruits of righteousness in your life today that will bring glory and praise to God?

Father, thank You for giving me, through You, the ability to love and bear fruit to Your glory. Help me to see the ways that I may do this today. Amen.

A Life that Advances the Gospel

Philippians 1:12

*"I want you to know, brothers, that what has happened to
me has really served to advance the gospel."*

The Philippians were concerned about Paul's well-being. They had not heard from him in almost two years, and then they got word that he had been imprisoned. They sent Epaphroditus to check on him and see how they might help. In reality, Paul was in prison. As a matter of fact, he was chained to a Roman guard 24 hours a day, but Paul's only concern in his corresponding letter to the Philippian church was that they rest in knowing that the gospel was being advanced.

Paul demonstrates what so many cannot fathom: The Christian life is not about a life concerned with self, about what will bring us fulfillment or the most pleasure. The Christian life is one of self-sacrifice where we continually say no to self and yes to those things that proclaim God's glory. Paul writes to reassure the Philippian church that what was most important – that the gospel was being proclaimed – was happening because of his imprisonment, so he and they were to rejoice in that. His reaction was not, "What is happening to me?" but "What is happening to the gospel?" As James Boyce puts it, "In one deft sentence Paul shifts the legitimate interests of the Philippians from himself to the great undeterred purposes of God in history." (*Philippians: An Expositional Commentary* [Zondervan], p. 60)

In all of our lives, let us focus not on the comforts of self and determine our joy from that, but let us take our example from Paul and make everything we do and the measure of the joy in those things dependent solely on the advancement of the gospel of Jesus Christ.

(continued)

– Study/Meditation –

In what ways can you improve your attitude when it comes to finding joy not in your circumstances but in the work of God in your life?

Father, forgive me for losing focus sometimes. Help me remember that all I do and all the measure of what I do is about You. Amen.

Are You Sharing the Gospel?

Philippians 1:13

"...so that it has become known throughout the whole imperial guard and to all the rest that my imprisonment is for Christ"

As stated yesterday, Paul was chained to a Roman guard 24 hours a day and the guards changed every four hours. His restriction was a complete one, and many of us might be tempted to think in terms of this restriction. However, Paul saw it as an opportunity to advance the gospel. Whereas we might think, "How limiting to his evangelism to be imprisoned like that," Paul thought, "What an opportunity to share Christ with these men who are with me every minute of the day!" These guards would have been accustomed to hardened criminals, men who had little or no concern for any humanity, much less the guards themselves. However, Paul was different. He asked about their families, prayed for them, and shared the love of Christ with them at every turn. Word spread throughout the Praetorian Guard about the gospel and this very different prisoner, and many of them believed. (Philippians 4:22)

We may often think that our vocations or our lives are devoid of ministerial opportunities because we are surrounded by unbelievers or because we aren't in "ministry." Paul would tell us that every area of our lives is to be seen as a place where Christ can be shared, and there are no such things as situations or people who prohibit our sharing the gospel.

– Study/Meditation –

With whom can you share the gospel this week? What has prohibited you from sharing with this person thus far? What might Paul tell you in terms of this seeming "prohibition"?

Father, help me to see where I might share Your love and the good news of salvation through Jesus with someone in my life. Thank You for those opportunities. Amen.

Living Examples

Philippians 1:14

"And most of the brothers, having become confident in the Lord by my imprisonment, are much more bold to speak the word without fear."

The Roman Christians were truly persecuted. They were scoffed at, ridiculed, and disrespected at every turn, and even more than that, their lives were in danger because of their Christian beliefs. They found themselves discouraged and fearful, often remaining quiet in the face of such peril. However, Paul once again demonstrated the clear and correct attitude after which we are to seek in our Christian walks, which is one of selfless endeavors toward proclaiming the glory of the Gospel of Jesus Christ.

Paul was in prison, and there he was continually speaking of salvation and the changing power of the blood of his Savior. As a result, not only were many of the prison guards coming to know the Lord, but his brothers and sisters in Rome who were witnessing his bold confidence while in chains were becoming more confident themselves. Consequently, they too were benefiting from Paul's unrelenting dedication to preaching the gospel.

Yes, unbelievers watch our lives. They will many times take their cues about Christianity from the way that we behave and the things that we say, and then we praise God when some of them come to know Him through those things. What we must remember is that our fellow believers are also watching, and when we persevere selflessly and in joy, looking ever forward to the eternity that awaits us, often they gain courage and strength from our lives. The Christ-centered life of a believer is an influential one, and it is in this that we remain ever diligent.

Read Colossians 3:12-17. How does this directive from Paul
to the Colossian church help us present good examples in
our lives for our fellow brothers and sisters?

*Father, thank You for Your saving grace. Help me to know better how I can
display Your majesty, glory, and love to all those around me. Amen.*

The Battle Against Self

Philippians 1:15-17

"Some indeed preach Christ from envy and rivalry, but others from good will. The latter do it out of love, knowing that I am put here for the defense of the gospel. The former proclaim Christ out of rivalry, not sincerely but thinking to afflict me in my imprisonment."

Paul's imprisonment was leading many to Christ, and it was emboldening some to preach the gospel more fearlessly. Unfortunately, some of that fearlessness was prideful and self-seeking. Some felt a boldness to preach now that Paul was out of the way, seeing it more as an opportunity to get in on what they saw as his influence or even his fame.

One of the saddest realities about humanity is its propensity toward self-exaltation. We are creatures of self. Without constant diligence, everything we do and think and say will be about our own comfort, happiness, and advancement. It is who we are naturally. Only by way of sanctification in Christ can we move out of our own way and place Him at the center of our lives and of our motivations in our lives.

Many apparently struggled with that during Paul's day. Many of us struggle with that today. As we move through our lives now, let us be aware of our propensity toward self-centeredness, while at the same time offering grace to our fellow brethren who struggle with the same things.

– Study/Meditation –

In what ways might you preach the gospel out of selfish ambition rather than to show the perfect glory and grace of God?
What should your response be to such things?

Father, forgive me for my selfishness. Thank You for giving me the Holy Spirit's influence in my life so that I have the avenue by which I can see beyond myself to You. Amen.

Fully Saturated with Christ

Philippians 1:18

"What then? Only that in every way, whether in pretense or in truth, Christ is proclaimed, and in that I rejoice. Yes, I will rejoice."

Paul had just told the Philippians that he was aware of the different men who were preaching the gospel while he was in chains. He knew that some of them did so out of love for Christ and that some did so out of vanity or rivalry with him. What was Paul's response? He literally asked, "So what?" He quite literally was so Christ-saturated and Christ-centered that his only concern was whether or not the gospel was being preached. Slander and false intentions could not deter him in his single minded goal of spreading the good news of Jesus Christ to everyone possible.

Furthermore, his response wasn't ambivalence to the cruel intentions and slander thrown his way. He wrote that as long as Christ was being preached, "In that I rejoice." His joy was a direct result of the proclamation of Christ's redeeming sacrifice. He said he rejoiced then, and that seeing and knowing that Jesus is preached will determine his joy in the future: "Yes, I will rejoice."

Do we have that kind of dedication to the Great Commission? Can we look past the sometimes cruel actions and intentions of others and how those things make us feel and live only in terms of Christ glorified? Let us come to the Throne of Grace over and over as we strive to be more like Paul, fully dedicated only to our Lord, with self securely out of frame.

– Study/Meditation –

Why do you think Paul could dismiss those who were preaching with wrong motives? How can you apply that to your life today?

Father, help me each day to look beyond my own feelings toward the only true purpose, which is to glorify You. Amen.

The Unquestionable Deliverance of God

Philippians 1:19

"(Yes, and I will rejoice), for I know that through your prayers and the help of the Spirit of Jesus Christ this will turn out for my deliverance."

Joy can sometimes be so slippery in this life, can't it? It slides down slopes of pain and heartache and loss, and then it shoots like a meteor when all is favorable and good. This sort of language and reality would have been nonsensical to the Apostle Paul, for his joy was consistent, no matter his circumstances, because it was founded on the Word of God. As long as "Christ is proclaimed" (v. 18), Paul says that he will rejoice. How? He does and will continue to be full of joy because he trusts God's Word as well as knowing it.

When he says that he knows that the prayers of the saints and Jesus Christ will invariably bring about his deliverance, he is quoting directly from Job 13:36. This is when Job prayed that he be delivered, or "saved," from the horrors he was facing because he knew the faithfulness of God. Whether Paul meant "saved" as in from prison or accusation or life, the point is that Paul trusted God's Word as well as knowing it. He rejoiced in knowing that his present trials and troubles were only temporary. Job was a righteous man, and the bible declares that God will deliver the righteous. (Job 36:7; Psalm 5:12, 34:15, 17) Paul knew that he had by imputation received the righteousness of Christ, and so he could be confident in his deliverance no matter the circumstance.

We should know and trust in this too, for this is the place of joy. This confidence and trust in our Father is the steady ground upon which we rejoice.

– Study/Meditation –

Using a concordance, do a word search of the word "righteous,"
looking for all of the places where God's Word declares that He will deliver
the righteous. Use this list in your study time every day as trials hit, taking
comfort from and trust in God's promises to deliver His children.

Father, thank You for giving me the gift of Jesus' righteousness,
which results in receiving Your deliverance. Amen.

18

Never Put to Shame

Philippians 1:20

*"As it is my eager expectation and hope that I will not be at
all ashamed, but that with full courage now as always Christ will be
honored in my body, whether by life or by death."*

Paul's trust in the provision and promises of God were unshakable, even in the face of death. He knew God's Word, and he knew that Jesus had said, "And I tell you, everyone who acknowledges me before men, the Son of Man also will acknowledge before the angels of God," (Luke 12:8) but that He also said, "Whoever is ashamed of me and of my words, him will the Son of Man also be ashamed when he comes in the glory of his Father with the holy angels." (Mark 8:38)

Paul had an earnest expectation, an unfaltering hope that he would never be disappointed by Christ, that Christ would never abandon nor let go of him. He knew that because he had been faithful to the gospel, that Jesus would not be ashamed of him and that he would never be left ashamed before man. Paul would have also known God's promise given in Isaiah 49:23, "Those who wait for me shall not be put to shame," even quoting this same verse in Romans 9:33. Imprisonment or defamation or torture or even death did not thwart Paul's unwavering trust in God's promise to be with him and to be faithful to His Word.

Do we rest like that today? In the midst of a scoffing world, can we believe and eagerly go forth, knowing that God will not let us be put to shame, no matter how things appear on the surface? Let us pray and live with these truths in mind, facing whatever perils come our way in this life with this same peaceful expectation and courage as is demonstrated in the Apostle Paul. God will not disappoint.

– Study/Meditation –

Read Isaiah 1:29, 45:17, 50:7 and Jeremiah 12:13.
What common thread runs throughout these Old Testament
promises? How does this bring you comfort?

*Father, I trust You. You are my Deliverer and my Rock and
my Strong Protector. You are ever faithful and trustworthy.
Thank You for choosing me. Amen.*

My Life is Christ

Philippians 1:21

"For to me to live is Christ, and to die is gain."

Basically Paul is proclaiming here that while he is breathing this air, his life is Christ, and when he breathes his last, that communion will be perfect and far better than he can even imagine now.

What does it mean to say that your life "is Christ"? It means that Jesus is your all in all, your all-sufficient One. It means that all that is true of Christ is all that is true for you. As Paul writes in Romans 6:10-11, "For the death he died he died to sin, once for all, but the life he lives he lives to God. So you also must consider yourselves dead to sin and alive to God in Christ Jesus." Truthfully, we need to grow in our understanding of this reality. We do so by actively communing with Christ and depending on Him for everything. We must grow to intimately know Christ (Philippians 3:10), to love Christ with all our heart, soul, mind, and strength (Mark 12:30), and we must submit all our thoughts, words, actions, and deeds to the lordship of Christ so that we seek only to please Him in all our lives (Colossians 1:10). In other words, the glorious person of Jesus Christ is, and nothing less, the Christian life.

This is a process, of course. Every believer has periods in his or her life where there is a struggle to live according to this wonderful reality. Paul writes that he had not attained it either (Philippians 3:12), but like him, we press on toward the goal of Christ because He has made us His. In this, our lives become more and more centered on our Savior.

– Study/Meditation –

What does it mean for you to practically, in your day-to-day life,
live a life that is Christ?

*Father, help me see the areas of my life where I am struggling
to live Christ, and give me the wisdom and discernment
to move more in line with my Savior. Amen.*

Life Defined by God

Philippians 1:22a

"If I am to live in the flesh, that means fruitful labor for me."

In order to truly understand what Paul is referring to in this verse, we have to look more closely at what he means by living "in the flesh" and why that "means fruitful labor" to him. In the previous verse, Paul had said that to him, "to live is Christ." In other words, if God's will was for him to continue living here on this earth, then his life would be all about Jesus; his life would be utterly defined by his Savior. The Apostle Paul had a crystal clear picture of what the Christian life is to look like, and his view of it should serve as a guidepost for the rest of us. Jesus said that others "will know that you are my disciples, if you have love for one another" (John 13:35), and that "every healthy tree bears good fruit." (Matthew 7:17)

Christians are to be defined by how our lives manifest Whose we are, and that manifestation is projected in the necessary results in these lives. Paul knew that if God ordained that he continue living on this earth that it wasn't to persecute him or punish him or leave him. If God orchestrated events so that Paul remained on earth a little longer, it was because He had work for Paul to do in His Kingdom. Paul would never have seen death as an escape or life as about his comfort. He accepted that God's perfect plan was indeed perfect, and that he would bear fruit to the glory of God for however long God desired. In this, God's ultimate and merciful sovereignty, Paul rested, and so should we.

– Study/Meditation –

How does Paul's attitude about life and death portray absolute peace in the sovereignty of God? How does this instruct you about your attitude today?

Father, thank You for keeping me in Your sovereign hand.
You are merciful and kind and just. Amen.

Where is True Joy?

Philippians 1:22b-24

"Yet which I shall choose I cannot tell. I am hard pressed between the two. My desire is to depart and be with Christ, for that is far better. But to remain in the flesh is more necessary on your account."

In these short sentences, Paul exemplifies what it means to be "in Christ" as described in verse 21. He has already written to the Philippian church in verse 18, "I rejoice. Yes, and I will rejoice." He was encouraging them even as he was near death and in chains that his joy remained, not because of his circumstances, but in spite of his circumstances. How? Because this man knew that joy is a state of mind that revolved around his Savior. This is a man of God whose entire focus was Christ.

He said in verses 22-24 that he was torn between two equally enticing desires – to either leave this world and so be with his Lord personally, or to stay in this world and continue steadfastly and joyously in His Lord's work. He didn't look to death with fear and angst; nor did he look to his life and wish for death. The point is that when we find our purpose in Christ, our situations – no matter what they are – do not constitute our joy in Him.

Our joy is in whatever serves and glorifies the One to whom we belong. When Jesus is your life, then your life can only bring joy. Doesn't that sound enticing? Don't we all wish for such contentment in the midst of pain and sorrow and death? If you answered yes to those two questions, then there is good news. There is no secret formula you must uncover or an exclusive club to which you must belong. If you are a Christian, then this life is available to you. You simply need to look to Christ, focus on Him, and live for Him. In short, then, you'll find constant joy in Him.

(continued)

Where is True Joy? – *continued*

– Study/Meditation –

What is your attitude about joy? How can Paul's attitude in his letter to the Philippians help you find the joy you seek now?

Father, thank You for the biblical examples we have such as Paul. Help me see the ways in which I can live now so as to know only joy in You and Your Son. Amen.

The Joy of Christ

Philippians 1:25-26

"Convinced of this, I know that I will remain and continue with you all, for your progress and joy in the faith, so that in me you may have ample cause to glory in Christ Jesus, because of my coming to you again."

What is ardently clear in verses 22-26 of Philippians 1 is that Paul's only and central concern was the advancement of the Gospel of Jesus Christ. Of course he would rather be with Jesus, but he equally wanted to remain with the church here on earth, so that through his work he could to build them up in order to bring more and more glory to God.

When he said, "Convinced of this," the language does not suggest that he had some supernatural revelation that he would escape death. More it suggests that he felt it deep inside, and that he had the abiding impression that his work on earth was not quite finished. However, instead of focusing on how or what Paul knew, it is so much more vital that we see on what and whom he was focused. Everything was about Christ for Paul, bringing His Savior glory and honor, and all to "progress and joy in the faith."

You see, Paul knew what so many of us either need to realize or at the very least, need to remember: The only avenue to joy is in sanctification and the advancement of the gospel in and through our lives. Paul loved the Philippians, and in this love he wanted them to experience peace and joy. He knew that Jesus was the only way to these precious states, so in his undaunted devotion to the gospel and love for his readers, he wanted from his life or death only those things that would serve to advance both. Do you seek joy today? If the answer is yes, then seek Jesus and seek to advance His glory, and joy will come. In fact, this is the only place where joy truly exists.

(continued)

The Joy of Christ – continued

– Study/Meditation –

Where do you typically seek joy in your life? In what ways can you either change those ways to be about Christ or alter them to be so?

Father, thank You for providing joy in my life through Your Son, Jesus Christ. Help me to see the ways in which I can advance Your glory through the gospel. Amen.

Citizens of Heaven

Philippians 1:27a

"Only let your manner of life be worthy of the gospel of Christ."

Philippi was a Roman colony, and the people there took pride in their Roman citizenship. Even though they were 800 miles from Rome, they answered to Roman authority; they followed Roman laws. Paul was speaking to their unique sense of citizenship. The phrase he used for "manner of life," also translated as "conduct yourselves," literally meant "live as citizens" in the original Greek. Paul was saying that no matter where we live geographically, we must conduct ourselves as citizens of our homeland, namely heaven.

Everything about the Christian life must mirror those things worthy of our Lord. We live to serve and please our King. It is inordinately sad when the church blends in with the world around it in matters of morality and behavior. Whereas we are called to be a part of the world so that we might share the gospel with it (1 Corinthians 9:20-23), we are to behave always as citizens of heaven, distinctly holy and set apart. As Paul stated elsewhere, we are to be ambassadors for Christ, representing the heavenly kingdom in all that we do. (2 Corinthians 5:20) After all, how can we draw others to the freedom only given in Christ if we are still living in bondage to the very same things from which we wish to see them freed?

– Study/Meditation –

Read Galatians 5:16-26. What does Paul say in this
letter about a life "worthy of the gospel of Christ"?

*Father, forgive me for the times when I do not live as one set apart as
holy unto You. Give me wisdom and discernment to see the areas in my
life where I must repent and live as a citizen of heaven. Amen.*

Destructive Competition

Philippians 1:27b

*"(Only let your manner of life be worthy of the gospel of Christ),
so that whether I come and see you or am absent, I may hear of you
that you are standing firm in one spirit, with one mind striving
side by side for the faith of the gospel."*

As humans, we are often prone to competition and individualism. These are certainly not bad traits, but they can be destructive, especially to unity within the church. When we don't see the value and necessity of "standing firm" and "striving side by side for the faith of the gospel," then we become one weak strand along with many other weak strands – easily broken and destroyed by the world and its deceptions. Together, however, we are woven into a strong chord, one that cannot be easily broken or frayed.

Paul was concerned that the Philippian church be able to stand against the persecutions and trials they were enduring and no doubt would continue to endure. When he used the word "striving," he was using the Greek word sunathleo from which we get our word "athletics." The picture is of an athletic team, working and striving together toward one common goal. That goal for the church is the "faith of the gospel."

The human characteristic of competition when applied to the church sets us against members of our own body, whether those members are worshipping with us in the same building on Sunday morning or in another gospel-centered gathering across town. Once again, when the center is Christ, then all need for goals focused on anything else fall by the wayside in favor of the advancement of His gospel.

– Study/Meditation –

Read what Paul wrote to the Roman church in Romans 12:3-8.
How does this passage relate to the truths Paul wrote in Philippians 1:27?

*Father, thank You for my local church and for the fellowship
of believers I have. Help me to see all the ways in which I can strive
together with them for the advancement of the gospel. Amen.*

No Fear

Philippians 1:28

"...and not frightened in anything by your opponents.
This is a clear sign to them of their destruction,
but of your salvation, and that from God."

It's amazing that sometimes Christians are surprised when people don't like them. However, the truth is that our service and devotion to our Savior and King will cause us to have enemies in this world. In many, many circles, religion and spirituality are perfectly acceptable topics, but the minute the name of Jesus enters the conversation, all bets are off!

Paul used a word that we translate as "frightened." It was used to describe a startled horse. Paul is basically saying the same thing he said in 1 Peter 4:12, "Beloved, do not be surprised at the fiery trial when it comes upon you to test you, as though something strange were happening to you." In other words, we shouldn't be frightened or surprised when people in the world don't like us, even to the extent that they become our enemies. The very idea of Jesus Christ stands boldly against all that is natural in fallen man. His place as King of kings and the only means by which man might be saved negates all pretenses that man can either make or find his own god. As a matter of fact, Paul assures us that when man opposes the Christ, "It is a sure sign of their destruction," while it is also a sure sign of our salvation.

We shouldn't be surprised at opposition because we expect it, and we shouldn't be frightened because we know that in Christ we have been promised eternity.

– Study/Meditation –

Read what Paul wrote in his beautiful Triumph Song, Romans 8:31-39.
How does this passage encourage you not to be afraid of those
who may stand against you in the name of Jesus?

*Father, thank You for giving me assurance in Jesus. Help me
to stand against those who are enemies of the cross
with this assurance without fear. Amen.*

Suffering for Faith

Philippians 1:29-30

"For it has been granted to you that for the sake of Christ you should not only believe in him but also suffer for his sake, engaged in the same conflict that you saw I had and now hear that I still have."

In many countries today, the fear in being a Christian lies in life and death. There is indeed religious persecution for the faith throughout this world, and many of our brothers and sisters heroically face that danger every day. However, for the most part, the fear of the Christian today isn't in physical danger, per se. The fear of the Christian in most parts of the world lies in the fear of ridicule, the fear that you may be seen as "foolish" and "radical" or even "racist" and "intolerant."

Paul faced both, as did the Philippian Christians to whom he wrote, and his words of comfort to them were the same Peter wrote in 1 Peter 4:13-14, "But rejoice insofar as you share Christ's sufferings, that you may also rejoice and be glad when his glory is revealed.

If you are insulted for the name of Christ, you are blessed, because the Spirit of glory and of God rests upon you." In other words, all suffering in the name of Christ is to be seen as a gift. Our Savior suffered all of it, from ridicule and slander to torture and death. We are certainly in good company. Christian, do not compromise your faith simply because you don't want to be seen as a foolish extremist. This suffering is also cause for rejoicing in that "it is a clear sign of your salvation." (Philippians 1:28)

– Study/Meditation –

In what ways have you suffered for being a Christian?
What was your attitude in the midst of that suffering?

*Father, thank You for including me in the things that prove
my salvation. You are my great and loving Lord. Amen.*

44

Encouragement in Christ

Philippians 2:1-2a

"So if there is any encouragement in Christ, any comfort from love, any participation in the Spirit, any affection and sympathy, complete my joy by being of the same mind…"

Paul had already stated that he will rejoice, no matter his circumstances, even though those circumstances were prison and being chained to a guard all day long. However, Paul's joy came from Christ and his position within Christ's kingdom. It's interesting here, then, that Paul asks the Philippian church to "complete" his joy. You see, he cared so much for this church that even his unshakable joy was somewhat incomplete without the Philippians believers understanding the beauty of unity in the body of Christ.

Paul asks them to complete his joy through the encouragement that only comes in Christ, the comfort that is only possible in His love, and the only unity that results from a participation in the Spirit. Our perspectives must be outside of this place, and our joy and affection and love must originate in Christ and in the Spirit so that disunity can find no place in our churches. If indeed we all saw reality in terms of eternity instead of in terms of our circumstances, like Paul did, then harmony would naturally occur in our relationships. Paul's love for these people could only be complete if they completed it through love for one another. How much more must our Savior desire that between His people?

– Study/Meditation –

Has there been any conflict(s) between you and someone in your church? Work today at reconciliation and peace in that relationship.

Father, forgive me my pride when it comes to others. Help me reconcile and live at peace, especially within my church family. Amen.

Living in Harmony

Philippians 2:1-2

*"So if there is any encouragement in Christ, any comfort from love,
any participation in the Spirit, any affection and sympathy,
complete my joy by being of the same mind, having the same love,
being in full accord and of one mind."*

One certain and abiding truth in life is this: Where there is more than one person gathered, there will be, even if only on occasion, disharmony. Humanity in its fallen state has a propensity toward self-centered behavior. After all, we can really only naturally see any situation from our own perspective. It takes effort and a full desire to deny this perspective in order to see from someone else's vantage point. Consequently, we rely on the abilities of Christ and the Holy Spirit in us to do so.

The Philippian church was a wonderful church and very dear to Paul's heart. However, they were dealing with some internal issues (4:2), which is understandable given that like all churches, it was "one body which has many members." (Romans 12:4) This church began with a sophisticated wealthy businesswoman, a Roman military soldier, and a young slave girl who had been into the occult. There was bound to be some friction! Paul was reminding them, as he is us, to look to what we have received in Christ – mercy, love, grace, and forgiveness – along with the guidance of the Holy Spirit in order to live in unity and harmony with our brothers and sisters.

Yes, it is difficult and sometimes painful, but the end result is a body that lovingly and purposefully demonstrates the glory of its Maker to a world that must see Him through them.

– Study/Meditation –

With whom in the body of believers do you struggle to live in harmony? In what ways will you seek do so?

Father, thank You for making me a member of Your body. Help me to live in harmony with them, forgiving and showing mercy as You have done for me. Amen.

The Secret to Joy and Contentment

Philippians 2:3

*"Do nothing from rivalry or conceit, but in humility
count others more significant than yourselves."*

If asked about the key to success, most people in the world would answer that it is found in self-fulfillment, self-satisfaction, or self-gratification. Of course, these premises would most likely be guised in other more acceptable and less self-centered words, but the essence would be the same. The truth is that it is human nature – "human," not "pagan," so this includes Christians – to seek happiness and contentment in life through means that ultimately elevate self, which is a direct result of pride and not humility. Non-Christian philosopher Allan Bloom saw this when he wrote, "Everyone loves himself most but wants others to love him more than they love themselves." (Bloom, "The Closing of the American Mind, 1987, p. 118)

Paul was warning the Philippian church that the only avenue by which they might attain true unity and joy is by humbly placing others first. A.B. Bruce wrote, "The whole aim of Satanic policy is to get self-interest recognized as the chief end of man." (Bruce, "The Training of the Twelve," 1897, p. 180) When we realize that our chief end is to "glorify God and fully enjoy Him forever" (Westminster Shorter Catechism), then we are freed from the bondage of self and thereby capable of moving toward the one and only thing that will bring true joy.

Our lives are not about what we can get out of them or how we can be uplifted by them. Our lives, as children of the Most High, must be about demonstrating the magnificence of our Father and in so doing finding joy that is both eternal and complete.

– Study/Meditation –

What does it mean in your life to place others first?

*Father, help me to see the areas in my life where
I need to grow in humility. Amen.*

The Golden Rule

Philippians 2:4

*"Let each of you look not only to his own
interests but also to the interests of others."*

Why is it that when the person in front of me at the checkout line has five more items than she should and writes a check when the sign clearly says "Cash Only," it's because she is inconsiderate, but when I do it, it's because I am in a hurry? Or why is it that when my spouse is late, it's because he hasn't managed his time appropriately, but when I'm late, it's because I have a lot on my mind?

The truth is that we only see things from our perspective and will then react from that single perspective unless we purpose ourselves to do otherwise. Paul is reminding us that we must condition ourselves to take others not only into consideration, but also to consider others first. Of course, this does not mean that we take on a sort of "door mat" mentality, where we consider only the needs of others. Even Jesus took time away from the crowd when He needed it (Mark 1:35-39). It is fully appropriate to consider our own needs. However, Paul is reminding us that our needs cannot be the only needs to which we look, nor should our perspective be the only one we see.

In other words, a Christian's view on life should be dictated by something that most of us learned as children in Sunday school: "So whatever you wish that others would do to you, do also to them." (Matthew 7:12) It seems simple, but it takes concerted effort. However, it is an effort that is born of the fruit of the Holy Spirit who gives us all we need in order to achieve it.

– Study/Meditation –

Why do you think it is so important to consider
others even as you consider yourself?

*Father, help me to see the needs of those around me
and to react appropriately to those needs. Amen.*

Perfect Humility

Philippians 2:5

"Have this mind among yourselves, which is yours in Christ Jesus...."

To what "mind" is Paul referring in this verse? He answered that question in verse 2, "Complete my joy by being of the same mind, having the same love, being in full accord and of one mind." In other words, Paul's goal is unity in the church, which he said in verses 3 and 4 is accomplished in selfless humility. Now Paul is giving us the supreme example by which we can attain this Christian unity – Jesus Christ.

Understand that we cannot emulate Christ's deity. We cannot copy His incarnation. We cannot perform His miracles or live His perfection. However, we can pattern our lives after His humility. Indeed He is our supreme example and model for this life, most especially in His humble service of others. After washing His disciples' feet in the upper room, Jesus said, "Do you understand what I have done for you? You call me Teacher and Lord, and you are right, for so I am. If I then, your Lord and Teacher, have washed your feet, you ought to wash one another's feet. For I have given you an example, that you also should do just as I have done to you." (John 13:12b-15) In the next few verses, Paul is going to explain exactly why we must look to the example given us by the King of kings as we live together in His name while on this earth, an example ensconced in perfect humility.

– Study/Meditation –

In your opinion, how important is unity among believers?
Why does Paul stress it so heavily?

Father, help me to be humble in both my attitude and my actions toward others.
Thank You, Jesus, for giving me the perfect example of how to do this. Amen.

The Central Message of Christianity

Philippians 2:6

"...who, though he was in the form of God, did not count equality with God a thing to be grasped."

Christianity carries an incredible message, one that goes unmatched by any other religion in the world. In India, people pray to a god so that he won't be angry with them, which consequently is true of every other religion in some form or another. But not in Christianity. Jesus Christ instead demonstrated the greatest form of humility in that He looked down on wretched humanity who hated Him and were His enemies and willingly yielded all privileges as God so that He could save them.

Paul begins his discussion of the great incarnation of our Lord by first establishing that He is, in fact, our Lord. When Paul says, "he was in the form of God," he used the Greek word morphe, which means "form." However, unlike the Greek word schema, which also means "form," one's morphe is unchanging. For example, my morphe is that I am female. I have been female since I was born and I will die that way. My schema, however, changes; I was an infant, then a little girl, and then an adult. Paul purposefully uses morphe because Jesus was, is, and always will be God – the "form" of God. But even so, our Lord Jesus didn't hold onto His position and the rights that go with it. Instead, He sacrificed them for us.

Our hope and our future lay in the unselfish, perfect humility of the incarnation of our Lord and Savior, Jesus Christ, and therein also lays our example of living with one another now – in humility.

– Study/Meditation –

Read John 1:1-5, 14. How did this apostle describe Jesus?

Father, thank You for Your Son, who willingly came to this earth in lowly humanity so that I might live. Thank You, Jesus, for Your sacrifice. Amen.

The Incarnation of Jesus

Philippians 2:7

"...but made himself nothing, taking the form of a servant, being born in the likeness of man."

Often Christians do not fully appreciate the complexities and the magnificence of the incarnation of Jesus Christ. This is one of those terms we use and honor, but those we sometimes do not fully understand or even contemplate. Paul almost forces the issue here, simply because really seeing what Jesus was willing to do exemplifies the most supreme example of humility we can ever be given.

What our Savior did was more than what is portrayed on a popular reality show today where the boss of an organization goes undercover to live the life of one of his employees. Jesus didn't go undercover. He "made himself nothing." In other translations, the text reads that he "emptied himself." He quite literally chose not to grasp or hold onto the privileges of His position as Lord and instead emptied Himself of those so that He could be our perfect sacrifice. Paul wrote that Jesus took "the form of a servant" and was "born in the likeness of man." Once again the apostle used the Greek word "morphe." Jesus literally became a servant and was born fully human, though certainly still fully God. He didn't just dress up like a servant and a man. He became those things so that He could, in perfect humility, be the propitiation we required for salvation. Our Lord truly is the most glorious model we could ever be given on how to live in humble servitude toward our brothers and sisters.

– Study/Meditation –

Read Isaiah 53. How exactly did your Savior humble Himself for your sake?

Father, I worship You in Your mercy and grace. Thank You, Lord Jesus, for Your humble sacrifice and Your love. Amen.

The Humiliation of Christ

Philippians 2:8

"And being found in human form, he humbled himself by becoming obedient to the point of death, even death on a cross."

It may seem at first glance as if Paul were repeating himself at the beginning of this verse, since he said in the previous verse that Jesus was "born in the likeness of man." However, Paul is taking us through a progression of thought so that we might see Christ's perfect humility in His sacrifice. It wasn't just that he became a man, that though He is God He still took on all of the weaknesses of human flesh, but the majority of people saw only that outward form. Most people didn't look on Him and see anything other than a mere man, calling him crazy and demon-possessed.

Can you imagine the humiliation to which He succumbed? He is the King of kings, and mankind largely didn't see it. But our Jesus didn't stop there. He continued by humbling Himself even further. He endured a mock trial where they spit on Him and beat Him and pulled out the hairs of His beard, all while He said not a word. He could have called down legions of angels and leveled the entire palace of the High Priest, but He remained quietly submitted to this humiliation – on our behalf. But again, He didn't stop there. Paul said that He suffered humiliation willingly "to the point of death, even death on the cross." Jesus humbly allowed the people He came to save to murder Him, and not just in any way. Paul used the word "even" because crucifixion, developed by the Persians and perfected by the Romans, was the most painfully excruciating death imaginable, reserved only for slaves and the worst of the riff-raff. He did that for you and for me. Oh, the amazing love of our God and Savior, and all so that you and I might know life.

(continued)

The Humiliation of Christ – continued

– Study/Meditation –

After reading Hebrews 2:5-18, why did Jesus
suffer and endure this level of humiliation?

*Father, please forgive me for when I under-appreciate what Your Son,
Jesus, did on my behalf. Thank You, Jesus, for Your loving sacrifice.
All praise and honor and glory unto Your Name! Amen.*

Christ is Lord

Philippians 2:9

*"Therefore God has highly exalted him and bestowed
on him the name that is above every name."*

One of the major assaults on the Christian faith is in questioning the deity of Jesus Christ. However, Paul lays this objection to rest as he continues his description of Christ's humility and of both what He was willing to give up for us and what is rightfully His from God, the Father. Paul begins this verse with "Therefore," which connects the coming thought with the previous statements. In other words, Paul is saying, "Because of Jesus' humble sacrifice, God has highly exalted him and bestowed on him the name that is above every name."

Notice that it is God who exalted Him. Jesus didn't exalt Himself, though He could have at any time. However, His humility and perfect sacrifice on our behalf was complete. Also notice that man didn't exalt Him. Man instead spit on Him and tortured Him, finally crucifying Him, even beneath a crude sign which named Him. Paul reinforced this thought as he spoke before the Sanhedrin in Acts 5:30-31, "The God of our fathers raised Jesus, whom you killed by hanging him on a tree. God exalted him at his right hand as Leader and Savior, to give repentance to Israel and forgiveness of sins." God, Himself, has given Jesus the "name above all names" – Yahweh – declaring Him as Lord. Any religion or person who denies the deity of Christ thereby denies not only what God's Word says, but also the very act of God in this exaltation.

– Study/Meditation –

Read Acts 2:33-36. How do both Paul's words as well
as the words of David lay testimony to Christ's deity?

*Father, thank You that my salvation is secured in Your Son,
Jesus Christ, whom You have exalted as Lord. Amen.*

Every Knee Will Bow

Philippians 2:10-11

"...so that at the name of Jesus every knee should bow, in heaven and on earth and under the earth, and every tongue confess that Jesus Christ is Lord, to the glory of God the Father."

The exaltation of Christ will be a fully complete and wholly absolute act by God. Truly, Christ has already been exalted to the right hand of God. He is seated on His throne even now. All Christians both know and attest to this biblical truth, but much of His created still resists confessing it. However, there will come a day when God will demand such proclamation, and it will come from every created being.

All creatures "in heaven" will bow and confess Jesus as Lord. This is no small statement. The angelic host are known to be mighty and powerful beings. The angel Gabriel struck such fear into Daniel that the man grew pale, lost all his strength, and could not speak. (Daniel 10:8, 10, 15) Likewise, every person "on earth" will bow and confess that Jesus is Lord. Many rulers and citizens of this planet willfully deny our Savior, even mock Him. God has made known that all of those men and women, both alive and dead, will partake in that glorious submission to Jesus' lordship on that great day when He returns. And finally, Paul reminds us that even those creatures "under the earth," that is the demons and beasts that follow Satan, will bow and confess Jesus as Lord. Again, this is no small statement; demons have been granted tremendous power on this earthly plain. The book of Job shows how Satan can move wicked people to commit slaughter, cause a powerful wind to knock down a house, and inflict a man with illness. (Job 1:15, 19, 2:7) Certain demons apparently have territorial power over entire nations (Daniel 10:13), but they, along with all other creation, will bow before our Savior and confess Him alone as Lord.

How is it that we should respect the power that has been granted demonic forces while acknowledging their ultimate submission to our Lord, who is for us and will never be against us?

Father, You are awesome and mighty to be praised! I acknowledge and glory in You and in my Redeemer, Jesus Christ, whom You have exalted. Amen.

Jesus Christ is Lord

Philippians 2:11

"...and every tongue confess that Jesus Christ is Lord, to the glory of God the Father."

Paul had just said in verse ten that "at the name of Jesus every knee would bow, in heaven and on earth and under the earth." To what are they going to bow? They will bow before His stance as Lord. When Paul wrote in verse nine that God had exalted Jesus and given him the "name that is above all names," that name is Lord. In the Septuagint, God's name is represented as "Lord." The reality now, then, is that Christ is known for what He has always been – God.

And what is even more perfect in this beautiful exclamation by Paul is that Jesus' exaltation as Lord brings his Father glory. God is actually glorified in the pronouncement of Jesus as God. How amazing is our Savior to have put these things aside so that He could come to earth as a man, with all things that come with such a lowly station, subject Himself to complete humiliation, and then only to be crucified on our behalf. This love is truly insurmountable and difficult to fathom, and yet He has given it to us.

One day every single person and being, both on earth and under the earth, will proclaim what you and I already know to be true: Jesus is Lord. Even so, come, Lord Jesus!

– Study/Meditation –

Read 1 John 5:20-21. What does the Apostle John proclaim that is like what Paul is proclaiming in Philippians 2:11? What does this mean to you in your Christian walk?

Father, thank You for sending Your own Son, who is Lord, to die so that I might live. Help me to live a life worthy of such a gift. Amen.

Diligent in Sanctification

Philippians 2:12

*"Therefore, my beloved, as you have always obeyed, so now,
not only as in my presence but much more in my absence,
work out your own salvation with fear and trembling."*

One of the most common misunderstandings among Christians is about the seemingly contradictory relationship between God's sovereignty and man's responsibility. Some believe that we just have to "let go and let God," where we feel no responsibility either in our own lives or in the furtherance of the gospel to change the lives of others. Still others live their lives thinking that it is entirely up to them as to whether or not they can earn a place in heaven, trying desperately to live lives worthy of getting a space there. The truth is that the balance between these two biblical truths is not "either/or" but "both/and". God is absolutely sovereign, and yet we are fully responsible, both in salvation and sanctification.

Paul's main message here is that we need to work out the practical implications of our salvation, because God Himself is working in our midst. We don't obey the Lord's commandments and strive toward a sanctified life to please anyone other than our Father, and we do so because we have a heart that has been changed to move in that desire. It is right and appropriate that we "work out" our salvation "with fear and trembling," because it is our responsibility "to walk in a manner worthy of the calling to which we have been called." (Ephesians 4:1)

Paul's admonition for all believers is sound: We must live today and every day with every effort toward sanctification. This is the proof and testimony to our changed hearts and new lives in Christ. Peter summed this up best in 2 Peter 1:10, "Therefore, brothers, be all the more diligent to make your calling and election sure, for if you practice these qualities you will never fall."

(continued)

Diligent in Sanctification – *continued*

– Study/Meditation –

Read all of the passage in 2 Peter 1:3-15. Why does
Peter say we must work out our salvation daily?

*Father, thank You for saving me. Help me to see each day the ways
in which I must work out this precious gift within my life. Amen.*

How Can We Obey?

Philippians 2:13

*"For it is God who works in you both to will
and to work for his good purposes."*

It is true that if we spend any amount of time looking in the mirror and reflecting on our own sinful tendencies, then the idea that we must "work out our own salvation" will bring the kind of fear and trembling that results in total immobility. And it should! As Paul has stated over and over in his letters, there is nothing in us that can result in the perfection required to enter into the Kingdom of Heaven. We are fully and completely stained creatures with no abilities for sanctification – on our own.

However, one of the most beautiful and gracious aspects of salvation is that we are made new. We are "new creations" (2 Corinthians 5:17), but as Paul went on to say in 5:18 of that letter to the Corinthian church, "All this is from God, who through Christ reconciled us to himself and gave us the ministry of reconciliation." Therefore Paul admonishes us to obey and work out our salvation, and then he encourages us that this is possible because God has transformed us. He has, in essence, given us Himself so that we have the means by which we can be sanctified.

How gracious and loving is our God in that He gives us what He requires! Consequently, we rejoice with our brother, St. Augustine of Hippo, who echoed what we all can thankfully pray: "Lord, command what you will, and grant what you command."

(continued)

39

How Can We Obey? – *continued*

– Study/Meditation –

How has God shown Himself faithful in your life by commanding you to obey and then supplying you with the means to do so?

Father, thank You that You have given me a new nature that aligns with Yours. Thank You for giving me all that I need so that I may work out my salvation according to Your will. Amen.

Complaining and Grumbling

Philippians 2:14-15a

"Do all things without grumbling or questioning, that you may be blameless and innocent, children of God without blemish in the midst of a crooked and twisted generation."

What is the chief end of man? The chief end of man is to glorify God and fully enjoy Him forever. (Westminster Shorter Catechism) However, when we complain and grumble in this life, we are doing everything other than bringing Him glory or enjoying Him in any respect. The truth is that grumbling and complaining are probably the most common of sins among Christians. As a matter of fact, we all do it so often that we may not even recognize it as sin. But it is sin, and it is sin against the sovereign majesty of our Father, which brings Him no glory whatsoever.

Basically when we complain about our circumstances or about the people in our lives or about our "lot" in this life, we are proclaiming for all who hear that we don't like what our Father has done and that perhaps He should have found a better way to handle our situations. We speak to the world who does not know God that we are saved by grace because of His great love, but then out of the other side of our mouths we complain as if that weren't enough. We grumble as if salvation and eternity and the love of the Creator God aren't quite sufficient.

What message are we sending to this "crooked and twisted generation" when we devalue God's gift of unmerited and undeserved eternal life by grumbling against the one we live now? Let us instead speak words of gratitude for the great gift we have been given in this present life that we live, bringing God His rightful glory and thereby proclaiming to a dying world that His way is the true and loving way.

(continued)

Complaining and Grumbling – *continued*

– Study/Meditation –

In what areas of your life are you more apt to
complain? How can you alter this response and
instead glorify God in your situation?

*Father, forgive me for the times that I grumble and complain. Help me
see Your majesty so that I might glorify You in all things. Amen.*

Lights in the World

Philippians 15b

"(...in the midst of a crooked and twisted generation),
among whom you shine as lights in the world."

Jess said during the Sermon on the Mount, "You are the light of the world....Let your light shine before others, so that they may see your good works and give glory to your Father who is in heaven." (Matthew 5:14, 16) The mission of the church, the mission of every Christian, is to both spread the Gospel to every nation and to shine as lights in a dark world, and if there is one thing we know for certain – this world is a dark place. The only hope it has is Christ, and the only knowledge it has of Christ is us.

Paul is simply reiterating something we all know to be true, and that is that the world is watching us. It is watching what we do, what we say, how we act. Paul was reminding the Philippians and us that we cannot become like the darkness. We, instead, have to be different. We have to shine the light of Christ to this world by being different. The trick is that the only way we can possibly be different is through Christ while we shine the light of Christ. This is only possible in Him, but the beautiful thing is that it is possible.

In short, be kind. Be compassionate. Be merciful. Be forgiving. Love as our Savior has loved. This is light and this is our mission.

– Study/Meditation –

Read Matthew 25:34-40; Luke 10:25-37; and Romans 12:20, 21.
What is the bible's clear teaching regarding how we are to treat others as
a light in a dark world? How can you do this practically this week?

Father, help me see the areas where I am to be a light in the world
around me. Show me specific ways that I can do this today. Amen.

Purpose and Sacrifice

Philippians 2:16

"…holding fast to the word of life, so that in the day of Christ
I may be proud that I did not run in vain or labor in vain."

One aspect of the changed heart for Christ is a desire to display this beautiful change for the entire world to see. Paul had just told us that we should stop grumbling and complaining as if God's gifts weren't enough, and to instead "shine as lights in the world." It's interesting that the next few phrases he uses in verse 16 give a couple of clues as to how we might do this as we wait expectantly for the return of our Lord, "the day of Christ."

First Paul says that we are to "hold fast to the world of life." The imagery created by the words he used portrays one who is holding onto something tightly while also holding it out for others to see or to partake in. There is always a danger when we seek to display anything by holding it out; we could drop it. Paul is warning us to keep a firm grasp on the truth of the gospel as we live it out in our lives, staying true to God's Word and being ever diligent to remain there so that we might not stray from it.

The next words he uses are "run" and "labor." He is writing in the context of our lives as shining lights in a dark world, and he means to give no illusion that this is somehow an easy thing to do. Candles burn brightly as they burn down. Lights shine in the darkness as they expend energy themselves. The Christian life was never meant to be an easy one, and once again Paul is reminding us that it is a life meant to be lived in self-sacrifice.

– Study/Meditation –

Why is it so important that believers firmly grasp
the gospel as they display it in their lives?

*Father, help me see the areas in my life where I need to
more abundantly shine the gospel forth. Help me also to
be more self-sacrificing in these areas so that
I may do so successfully. Amen.*

Service to Christ

Philippians 2:17-18

"Even if I am to be poured out as a drink offering upon the sacrificial offering of your faith, I am glad and rejoice with you all. Likewise you also should be glad and rejoice with me."

The idea of "sacrifice" has all but lost its truest meaning in modern day society. We often think that we sacrifice if we go without a few dollars so that we can drop it in the offering plate on Sunday, or when we give up a few hours of our time to make someone a meal or help them move their furniture. We've defined "sacrifice" as giving up something of value for a time so that we can give that portion of value to someone or something else. However, Paul and the Philippian church had in mind a different kind of sacrifice.

When Paul said that being "poured out as a drink offering upon the sacrificial offering of your faith" brings him joy, the image he was creating and the Philippians were receiving was of blood and death upon a stone altar. Paul rejoiced in his life – not his death – being the final culmination of the sacrifice, or the drink offering, bringing all glory and honor to Jesus Christ.

The idea of a sacrificial life in the sense in which Paul was speaking is often foreign to us, but it shouldn't be. As a matter of fact, one of the reasons so many Christians live outside of the joy that is rightfully theirs is because they live by seeking joy in possessions or people rather than in true sacrifice for Christ. How many of us are exhilarated with joy in the sacrifices we make for the cause of Christ?

– Study/Meditation –

How do you really define "sacrifice" in terms of your life for Christ? How is God calling you to sacrifice for Him?

Father, forgive me for my sometimes shallow view of living a sacrificial life. Help me to see the areas where sacrifice is necessary on behalf of Your Kingdom. Amen.

44

Rejoicing Together

Philippians 2:18

"Likewise you also should be glad and rejoice with me."

What exactly was Paul writing to the Philippians when he told them they should be rejoicing with him as he rejoiced, even in his trials? Once again, Paul is talking about unity amongst believers, in this case, sharing the act of rejoicing in all circumstances, not just our own. Paul knew the wonder and beauty of fully trusting in Jesus while he was in good situations and in bad. That's why he wrote later in this letter, "I have learned in whatever situation I am to be content." Basically he was saying that life itself had taught him to trust God. Naturally he wanted this same peace for his fellow brothers and sisters in Christ. Consequently, he admonished them to share in his contentment and his joy, even in his troubles.

We often mistakenly try to pray ourselves out of our troubles instead of praying ourselves through them. The bad times in our lives are not there to make us miserable; they are there to mature us, to prepare us, and to bring us ever closer to our Savior. Otherwise we run the risk of becoming self-sufficient and self-satisfied. Paul knew that peace only exists when we give Christ full reign in our lives, understanding that the plan God has for us is for our good and to His glory. Romans 8:28 is in every bible translation. It's in yours, too, and it's there for a purpose. May each of us truly comprehend the magnitude of what Paul wrote there, as well: "And we know that for those who love God all things work together for good, for those who are called according to his purpose."

– Study/Meditation –

Read Jeremiah 29:11-13. What truths can you see in these
verses about God and about our responsibilities?

Father, thank you for all things that happen in my life, both good and bad.
Help me to be mindful that You are in control, and that everything that
happens only does so because You have deemed it best for me. Amen.

Full Submission

Philippians 2:19

"I hope in the Lord Jesus to send Timothy to you soon, so that I too may be cheered by news of you."

In the next section of Paul's letter to the Philippian church, he is going to speak of the two men who were with him in Rome as he was writing, two men who exemplify what it means to be a follower of Christ – these men were servants. There is a church in Santa Fe, New Mexico, that has a sign over the only door to the church that reads, "Servant's Entrance." Every member of that church is considered a servant of Christ and of the body of believers, and Timothy and Epaphroditus were wonderful examples for us on what this looks like.

As Paul begins his introduction with Timothy, however, he first gives us another, vital characteristic of a believer, and that is total submission to God's will in his or her life. Paul says that he hopes "in the Lord" to send Timothy to the Philippians. Everything Paul did and thought was encapsulated in the knowledge that God is sovereign and that his life was ultimately in his Father's hands. Paul submitted all his plans to the Lord, and this is precisely what we must do.

What that means is that we make plans and we create strategies and we set goals, but they are all subject to the sovereignty of the Lord under whose leadership we live. We are not mindless robots under the direction of a cosmic puppet master, but we are subject to our Master's sovereign will. We live as those who know for knowing that we have a loving Father who perfectly leads us into the paths of righteousness, who has plans for us, "plans for wholeness and not for evil, to give us a future and a hope." (Jeremiah 29:11)

– Study/Meditation –

What does it look like to practically make plans and strategies
in this life while submitting to God's sovereign will?

*Father, thank You that You only will what is good for me and
what will bring You glory. Thank You that You have made plans
for me and that those plans will come to fruition.
Thank You for that kind of love. Amen.*

Be Genuine and Sincere

Philippians 2:20-21

"For I have no one like him (Timothy), who will be genuinely concerned for your welfare. They all seek their own interests, not those of Jesus Christ."

If asked why they refuse to attend or to become a member of a church, most non-believers give hypocrisy as their reason. What they unfortunately see is a lack of genuineness, a lack of sincerity, and because of this, there is no foundation for trust with their hearts. We can't really blame them. Sharing one's burdens and lives with another requires inordinate trust. Paul is holding Timothy up in these verses as an example of true servanthood and humility, and his first means of doing so was to point to the genuineness of Timothy's character.

Timothy wasn't putting on an act. He wasn't looking for a position in the church or a means by which he might advance himself. As a matter of fact, Paul is quick to point out that Timothy wasn't like many of the other people who were putting on the face of a servant but who were really only doing so with ulterior motives. Timothy, Paul says, was "genuinely concerned" for the Philippians' welfare. In other words, Timothy exemplified what Paul already wrote in 2:3, "Do nothing from rivalry or conceit, but in humility count others more significant than yourselves."

Christians are to be about the work of the King, and they are to do so with love and compassion born from a changed and sincere heart. This is not just the work of those in ministry. This is the work – it is the mission – of every believer.

– Study/Meditation –

In what ways can you be a true servant
in your church this week?

*Father, help me to see the places where I might
serve genuinely in my church and in my
community in Your name. Amen.*

47

Serving in Humility

Philippians 2:22-24

"But you know Timothy's proven worth, how as a son with a father he has served with me in the gospel. I hope therefore to send him just as soon as I see how it will go with me, and I trust in the Lord that shortly I myself will come also."

The very essence of the word "servant" implies considering one's self after another or even lower than another. It denotes the necessary characteristic of denying one's own desires for standing or position in order to serve another. However, as Timothy exemplified, it also requires a willingness to serve not only alongside of another, but in many instances, a willingness to humbly serve under the authority of another. Timothy had "proven worth." He had obviously suffered hardships associated with this willingness, and yet he served selflessly and without regard to either himself or a need for position. Consequently, Paul trusted him and wanted to send this faithful servant in his stead to minister to the Philippians until the apostle himself might possibly join him.

Jesus taught that it should be our inclination to seek the lower position and serve without desiring acclamation. He taught the lesson of the one who came to a dinner party and immediately sat at the head of the table and who was consequently embarrassed when he was asked to move down in favor of a more important guest. Instead, He said that we should assume the place of less importance so that in our humility we will receive honor. (Luke 14:10) Are you serving today in that kind of attitude?

– Study/Meditation –

Read all of Luke 14:7-11. What is the important lesson Jesus is teaching in this parable?

Father, forgive me when I think of myself more highly than I ought. Please give me opportunities to serve in the humility that honors You. Amen.

48

Greatness in God's Eyes

Philippians 2:25

*"I have thought it necessary to send to you Epaphroditus
my brother and fellow worker and fellow soldier, and
your messenger and minister to my need."*

We know little about this man Epaphroditus from biblical accounts, but we can ascertain pieces of his character from this brief description in Paul's letter to the Philippian church, a description that underlines Paul's holding him up along with Timothy as an example of humble Christian service. Paul calls Epaphroditus his "brother," using a term in Greek that meant more than just spiritual brothers. It carried with it a feeling of camaraderie, affection, and friendship. Epaphroditus was very special to Paul and they had a very close relationship.

Secondly, Paul called him his "fellow worker." Here the apostle is stressing Epaphroditus' laboring alongside of him in the work of Christ. This close brother was also a close and equal laborer.

Then Paul refers to him as a "fellow soldier," which was a very honorable title. This same reference was made in Greek culture to honor a common soldier as equal to the commander-in-chief or to the general. Basically, Paul was lifting Epaphroditus up to the Philippians as equal to himself in their mutual battle against a spiritual adversary.

Indeed, this was a unique and amazing man. And yet with all of these truly inspiring characteristics, Epaphroditus was a "messenger" and a "minister" to Paul's needs. He was, quite simply, a humble servant. How complete is this picture of Christian servitude from a man who could have seen reason to elevate himself given his nature and qualities, but who instead chose a life of service to his Christian brothers and sisters. We should indeed take much from this example and live our lives with this kind of attitude.

(continued)

Greatness in God's Eyes – *continued*

– Study/Meditation –

What are some practical implications you can take from this description of Epaphroditus about how you must live your own life?

Father, give me a heart to serve like that of Epaphroditus. Help me see the areas where I can improve and the places where I must step out and serve like this. Amen.

Others More than Ourselves

Philippians 2:26

*"For he (Epaphroditus) has been longing for you all and
has been distressed because you heard that he was ill."*

Paul is writing to the Philippians that he is going to send Epaphroditus to them, this man who was invaluable to the apostle in ministry. Why? The answer is another testimony to the kind of man this Epaphroditus truly was. He had been "longing" for his Philippian brothers and sisters, but Paul wasn't sending him to them because he was homesick, though perhaps he was. That would have made for a weak servant, one who was perhaps a little immature in his abilities to serve with Paul in the kingdom-work. No, Paul went on to say that Epaphroditus was "distressed," which was a word used to describe someone who was deeply and inordinately grieved. It was the same word Jesus used in the Garden of Gethsemane in Matthew 26:38, "My soul is deeply grieved to the point of death."

But even more telling of the extraordinary character of Epaphroditus was the reason for this deep grief. He was distressed because the Philippians heard that he was ill. In a world where mankind is naturally preoccupied with self, it is a rare thing for a man to be so "other-centered" that his very own illness doesn't grieve him as much as having those he loved worried over his illness.

It becomes easier and easier for us to see why Paul held these two men – Timothy and Epaphroditus – up as wonderful examples of what he wrote earlier that we are to humbly "count others more significant than yourselves." (Philippians 2:3)

(continued)

Others More than Ourselves – *continued*

– Study/Meditation –

In what ways can you emulate men like
Epaphroditus in your daily walk?

*Father, thank You for examples like Timothy and
Epaphroditus in Your Word. Help me to see daily how
I might follow these great men in my own walk. Amen.*

Concern for Others

Philippians 2:27-28

"Indeed he (Epaphroditus) was ill, near to death. But God had mercy on him, and not only on him but on me also, lest I should have sorrow upon sorrow. I am the more eager to send him, therefore, that you may rejoice at seeing him again, and that I may be less anxious."

There is a magnificent thing that we can glean from this short exchange between Paul and the Philippian church concerning the apostle sending Epaphroditus back to them. Notice that the Philippians were grieved when they heard that Epaphroditus was ill, Epaphroditus was grieved because the Philippians were concerned for him, and Paul was grieved because both Epaphroditus and the Philippian church were distressed about each other. No one was concerned about himself, but everyone was concerned for everyone else. This is the truest picture of humility and Christian brotherhood.

We see here an amazing picture of the regenerated heart in action, manifesting both service and love toward one another. And right in the middle of this concern and humility is the Lord. Paul very fluidly mentions that it was God who had mercy on Epaphroditus and upon all of them in sparing the man's life so that they might be spared "sorrow upon sorrow," or "wave upon wave of grief." What we see exemplified here is our Father in the center of His people who are giving Him all glory while they selflessly looked to the cares and concerns of their brethren. What we see here is a beautiful picture of the church.

– Study/Meditation –

How do you see the interaction between Paul, Epaphroditus, and the Philippians as a perfect example of how your own church should be? What examples have you seen in your church of this behavior?

Father, thank You for placing me in Your family. I lift up to You my fellow brothers and sisters and ask that they know Your boundless and unending love and security. Amen.

Sacrifice

Philippians 2:29-30

*"So receive him in the Lord with all joy, and honor such men,
for he nearly died for the work of Christ, risking his life to
complete what was lacking in your service to me."*

"Honor" and "respect" are valued words in our society, but for what do we bestow such things on a man or woman? Paul instructed the Philippians to honor Epaphroditus when he returned to them and to "receive him in the Lord with all joy," and he instructed them to do so because of the sacrificial life Epaphroditus led. These sacrifices nearly cost the man his life, and some of the words Paul used shed light on the significance of his service. When Paul said that Epaphroditus had been "risking his life," he was using words that pertained to gambling, rolling the dice, or in this case, exposing one's self to danger. That's what Epaphroditus did. He was so loving and so loyal that he willingly gambled with his own life so that he could both serve Paul and the Philippians.

We live in a society today that is all about safety and security, even for the believer. We accept Jesus as our Savior and then we're safe; heaven awaits. Afterwards, we go about our lives making sure that we don't have to risk health or well-being, working toward a comfortable living where we don't worry about our futures here either. In essence, we live lives dedicated to self-fulfillment, which is absolutely counterproductive to all that God has called us. On the contrary, we have been called to give our lives away for the cause of Christ and in humble service toward others in sacrifice. What are you risking today in the name of your Lord and for someone else?

– Study/Meditation –

Think on ways that you can actively live sacrificially in the name of Christ and make it a goal to act on at least one of those ways this week.

Father, help me see where You would have me sacrifice for Your Kingdom and on behalf of others. Amen.

Our Sure Weapon

Philippians 3:1

"Finally, my brothers, rejoice in the Lord. To write the same things to you is no trouble to me and is safe for you."

Very seldom do we believe the lies of the enemy on his first attempt at deception. Of course, there are exceptions to this statement, but by in large, it is true. Satan knows that, so his tactics are more often than not slow and meticulous, giving us just a bit of it at a time. Eventually, if we aren't bolstered against such deceptions, they appear not so bad, and then even correct.

Paul is about to re-iterate to the Philippians that salvation is by faith and not by ceremony or ritual or the law, and he begins the section by telling them that it doesn't bother him one bit to repeat himself. As a matter of fact, he said it "is safe for you." Why is that so? These words are sound because Paul knew that the enemy is methodical in his deception, so we must be likewise methodical in our defense.

This methodological defense is in repetitive study of and meditation on God's Word. It's in listening to and following sound teaching that is centered on God's Word. And finally, it's in following the advice and counsel of those who are speaking the truth of God's Word. When flood waters rise, they will eventually overtake a solitary levy or dam unless that barrier is bolstered consistently, not only to match the waters but to supersede their heights. This is what we must do in regards to the lies perpetrated by Satan. We bolster our levy of truth so that they not only match his lies, but that they are far in a way higher and stronger than anything he might throw our way.

Read Romans 12:1-2. How does Paul say
we should bolster our levies of truth?

*Father, thank You for Your Word that strengthens
and secures me against the lies of Satan. Amen.*

The Answer

Philippians 3:2

"Look out for the dogs, look out for the evildoers,
look out for those who mutilate the flesh."

The false doctrine about which Paul was warning the Philippian church is the same false doctrine still infiltrating the church today – that human merit or effort must come alongside of Jesus' work on the cross in order to facilitate salvation. Paul felt so strongly about these false teachers and the devastating effect they were having on the gospel, that he used very strong language in reference to them, which most assuredly got their attention. He called them "dogs" and "evildoers" and "those who mutilate the flesh," all of which were intentional slurs against the Judaizers. These Judaizers often called Gentiles "dogs" because they had no prejudices in the food they ate, whether it was clean or unclean. They likened them to the wild dogs that ate the city garbage. Paul called the Judaizers "dogs" instead.

The Judaizers were also known for their so-called "good works," which were nothing more than the ceremonies and rituals they tried to impose on everyone. Paul called them "evildoers" as opposed to "doers of good." And finally, the Judaizers were claiming that the Gentiles must also be circumcised to be a Christian, just as they were, so Paul called them the opposite – "mutilators of the flesh."

Paul's point was clear: Anything that leads us away from the absolute and complete work of Christ unto salvation by deleting or adding to it is opposed to our Savior's perfect righteousness and the imputation of that onto His followers. In short, Jesus is the only answer to our sin.

What can you do today to heed the Apostle Paul's
warning to "Look out" for false teachings such as these?

*Father, give me the discernment I need to see past
and through anything that might diminish or negate
the perfect work of Christ on my behalf. Amen.*

What is Real Circumcision?

Philippians 3:3

"For we are the real circumcision, who worship by the Spirit of God and glory in Christ Jesus and put no confidence in the flesh."

The Judaizers were infiltrating the church, attempting to convince the Christians there that in addition to accepting the saving blood of Jesus Christ as a means for their salvation, they also had to perform certain ceremonies and rituals to make their salvation complete. One of the main rituals they were advocating was circumcision. Paul refutes that teaching by saying that believers who rely solely on the imputation of Christ's righteousness for salvation are the "real circumcision," in that they have been reborn fully in Jesus. Paul says that true Christians "put no confidence in the flesh," but only in the Holy Spirit and the glory of their Savior.

Today there are many who are deluded into thinking they must add to the work of Christ in order to secure their salvation, both by works and by flesh. Yes, trying to earn one's way into heaven by good works is certainly one way that mankind tries to add to Christ's atonement for sins, but we also attempt to do so by the so-called "self-esteem movement." Often Christians are coerced into making happiness and fulfillment about more than Jesus, feeling that their self-worth is tantamount to reaching this joy. "You can do it" or "You're great" take the place of "Jesus is my all in all." Nothing – not things or persons or self – can do what only Jesus has done on our behalf. Thinking otherwise is not only bondage to a lie, it is blasphemous to the lordship of our Savior.

– Study/Meditation –

Read Jeremiah 17:5-8. What does the prophet Jeremiah record God as saying about putting confidence in the flesh instead of in Him?

Father, forgive me when I look to anything other than the saving blood of Jesus for my security in eternity. I know that You have given me all that I need in Your Son for my salvation. Amen.

Good Enough?

Philippians 3:4-7

"Though I myself have reason for confidence in the flesh also. If anyone else thinks he has reason for confidence in the flesh, I have more: circumcised on the eighth day, of the people of Israel, of the tribe of Benjamin, a Hebrew of Hebrews; as to the law, a Pharisee; as to zeal, a persecutor of the church; as to righteousness, under the law blameless. But whatever gain I had, I counted as loss for the sake of Christ."

God's Law can be compared to a ten-link chain that holds a boat to a dock. It only takes one broken link to cause the boat to be swept away by the current and broken to pieces against the shore. Some people who have behaved pretty well over all may look at a person who has broken just about every link in the chain and think, "At least I'm better than she is!" But one broken link is enough to plunge the entire boat into destruction. That's exactly what Paul had concluded in Romans 3:23, "For all have sinned and fallen short of the glory of God."

The truth is that in order to enter heaven on our own merit, we must maintain an unbroken chain of obedience from the moment we take our first breath until the moment we take our last. We must be perfect as our Father in heaven is perfect. (Matthew 5:48) Paul was making this point in these verses as he reiterated his own stellar example of "rule-following," one that would make any good Jew sit up and take note. However, even that record was "counted as loss for the sake of Christ." Even that record, Paul was saying, would not stand and be reckoned as anything compared to the perfection offered up for us in Jesus Christ. Would yours?

(continued)

Good Enough? – *continued*

– Study/Meditation –

What "merits" are you still holding onto in an effort to earn
your place in heaven? How must you release those?

*Father, thank You that I do not have to maintain an unbroken
chain of obedience to enter into eternity, but that You have sent
Your own Son to be what I could never be on my behalf. Amen.*

No Weights and Measures

Philippians 3:8

"Indeed, I count everything as loss because of the surpassing worth of knowing Christ Jesus as my Lord. For his sake I have suffered the loss of all things and count them as rubbish, in order that I may gain Christ."

Pride can sneak up on us in a myriad of ways. It may be that we feel really proud of our dedication to our devotional time, or maybe we hold in high esteem our efforts toward righteous behavior. Many of us get to the end of each day with an imaginary ledger in our heads where we measure how many gold stars are on the "Good Christian" side and red X's on the "Bad Christian" side. If we see in our heads more gold than red, then we sleep peacefully, feeling that we did a good job that day.

Self-righteousness and self-sufficiency are extremely slippery slopes, and unless we adopt Paul's attitude toward anything outside of Christ, we run the risk of adding our efforts to His finished work. Paul wrote that he counted anything and everything that may be human effort as "rubbish" alongside of knowing Christ as his Lord. That word "rubbish" can be translated as "dung." That's how far apart this apostle saw his merit from the person of Jesus. He instead realized that "knowing Jesus as my Lord" is of "surpassing worth" – not Jesus as his family's Lord or his tribe's Lord or his country's Lord, but as his personal Savior.

Nothing any man or woman will ever do can even stand in the shadow of Jesus, so why would we ever try to add our effort to His perfection?

(continued)

No Weights and Measures – continued

– Study/Meditation –

Read Romans 3:9-20. How does Paul explain our merit alongside of Christ's perfect righteousness in his letter to the Romans?

Father, thank You for the finished work of Jesus for my salvation. Thank You that He is my Savior. Amen.

Two Ways to Heaven?

Philippians 3:9

"...and be found in him, not having a righteousness of my own that comes through the law, but that which comes through faith in Christ, the righteousness from God that depends on faith."

Many think that there are only two ways to enter into heaven, and even if there were, one of them never works. The way that never works is the way by our own merit. That way requires perfection. It requires an unimpeded absolute keeping of every one of God's laws from the moment we take our first breath to the moment we take our last. The other way is Jesus, and He is the only way where fallen man can ever enter into the Kingdom of God. When our faith is placed in Jesus as our Savior, His righteousness – a righteousness that we can never attain on our own since it is perfect – is immediately imputed to us. In other words, His perfection is moved onto our accounts ledger, wiping out all of the red that existed there without Him. God, then, sees us only through His Son's righteousness, which enables us to stand before Him where we would otherwise perish in the presence of His holiness.

Paul says we are "found in Him" so that all that is true of Christ becomes true of us. At the instant we abandon all trust in our own good works and place that trust in the person and work of Jesus Christ, we are placed in Him. We are justified. In Him we are blessed with every spiritual blessing in the heavenly places. (Ephesians 1:3) There are only two ways into heaven, and one of them never works. The good news is that the other One always does.

– Study/Meditation –

What does it mean that Christ's righteousness is "imputed" to us when we place our faith in Him for salvation? (Hint: Read Romans 5:1-11).

Father, I praise Your holy name, and I thank You for giving me a way to live in eternity. Thank You for Your grace. Amen.

Sharing in the Sufferings of Christ

Philippians 3:10

"...that I may know him and the power of his resurrection, and may share his sufferings, becoming like him in his death."

"One of the most dangerous forms of human error is forgetting what one is trying to achieve." (Paul Nitze, Readers Digest, 7/92, pg. 37) Although said from a worldly perspective, this is also true of Christians. We must keep ever before us the purpose of our salvation and the reasons we live now, and this will only be true if we are vigilant in our relationship with Christ. Paul said that he sought to be known in the righteousness of Christ so that he might "know Him." When we seek to really know Jesus, we will necessarily know the "power of His resurrection," or the magnitude of what He accomplished on our behalf when He was raised from the dead. He defeated death so that in His sacrifice He procured eternal life for all those who accept His lordship.

In this knowing Him, we also "share His sufferings, becoming like Him in His death" when we suffer the temptations and sins of this life, dying to self so that in Him we might live. And all of this so that we do not lose sight of what we are going to achieve, pressing on "toward the goal for the prize for the upward call of God in Christ Jesus." (Philippians 3:14) We seek to know our Savior, to live in Him and by Him as we share in His sufferings due to sin so that we might become more like Him, keeping our eyes ever fixed on the prize of eternal life, thereby defeating death. Let us not forget where we are going as we strive on the path of getting there.

– Study/Meditation –

Read Jesus' prayer in John 17:1-26. What do Jesus' own words tell you about what we must know about Him and what He desires for us?

Father, help me to see the ways in which I must share in Christ's sufferings so that I might become more like Him. Amen.

A New Life

Philippians 3:11

*"..., that by any means possible I may attain
the resurrection from the dead."*

As I was driving the other day, I found myself behind a truck with the following slogan plastered across its rear window: "HELLBOUND." The sadness is tremendous that some people on the earth today think that is something about which they should brag, but even more than that is the ignorance about what that end will actually bring. As believers, however, do we long for our awaited "resurrection from the dead" with the passion that Paul did? Do we live each day on earth, not as if this is our reward, but as those who know that the rewards still await us on that great and glorious Day when our Savior returns to take us home?

Paul had taken inventory of his life – all of his achievements and man-centered calls for glory – and found that all of it meant nothing outside of Christ. He could only do so because everything about him was so Christ-centered and eternity-centered that perspective wasn't an issue. He knew what he wanted more than anything, and he desired that his readers long for the same thing – eternity with Jesus.

Only when we look past where we are and what is going on in our lives now to the hope of eternal glory we know we have in our Lord can we truly long for our eternal home. This takes an eternal perspective, one where we see beyond this world to the one that waits for us. Let's pray today that we can sing with Paul these words from Philippians 3:11: "By any means possible, I long for the resurrection from the dead so that I might live forever with my Lord."

(continued)

A New Life – continued

– Study/Meditation –

Do you long for heaven? Why or why not? What might you do so that you can gain the eternal perspective needed to long for your home with Jesus?

*Father, thank You for the promise You've made to bring
me into glory to live forever. Help me see that truthfully
so that I live in the joy of what awaits me, not in the
disappointments I may experience here. Amen.*

The Christian Race

Philippians 3:12

"Not that I have already obtained this or am already perfect, but I press on to make it my own, because Christ Jesus has made me his own."

As Paul continues his plea with his Philippian readers to live in Christ, seeking to know Him fully, he spends the next few verses using a racing analogy. He likens the Christian and his or her life on this earth to a runner in a race who presses on to the goal of eternity. This may seem like an obvious statement, but many people alive today are trying desperately hard to run a race they haven't even entered yet. They work and work at living what they see as a Christian life, pressing on as it were, trying to make this life their own, but they have never given their lives over to the Lordship of the One they are running toward.

Paul already used himself as one such example. (3:4-6) He worked hard. He was sincere. He was diligent and dedicated and zealous. However, there was one big problem: he wasn't genuinely converted to Jesus Christ. He could only claim that he was in the race 25 years later as he wrote this letter to the Philippians, as he claims, "Because Christ Jesus made me his own." Paul's conversion on the road to Damascus was the moment where Jesus reached down and literally brought Paul to Himself. The decision was Christ's. It always is, and then the decision rests in the hands of the one chosen. What a marvelous peace we have when we understand we're in this race because we were called out to be so.

– Study/Meditation –

Several times in the New Testament, the racing analogy
is used. Read 1 Corinthians 9:24-27 and comment on
Paul's point in this text when using this analogy.

Father, help me to see how it is that I must "press on" toward the goal of eternity. Thank You for choosing me to be in this race toward You. Amen.

The Marathon

Philippians 3:13-14

"Brothers, I do not consider that I have made it my own. But one thing I do: forgetting what lies behind and straining forward to what lies ahead, I press on toward the goal for the prize of the upward call of God in Christ Jesus."

The Christian life isn't a 100-yard dash; it's a full marathon, and we must live it with a mindset of pressing on as Paul describes in these verses. One of the biggest issues for many Christians today is that we live in the land of "quick fixes." We've lost sight of patience and endurance in our society of 30-second meals and drive through pharmacies. We want it all, and we want it now! That is not the method by which our Father has given us to live this life while on this earth.

Paul said that he knew he had not made it to the finish line, that he wouldn't make it to the finish line until he went home to be with his Father, and so he therefore never stopped working at this life while he lived it. He used the phrase "straining forward," which denotes an image of a runner stretching forward toward the finish line. He knew he was still running this race, but his only goal was to finish well. Take note, however: his goal was in straining toward the goal of Christ, not in getting what he might want while here.

This life isn't a sprint, so we have to run it like an endurance runner, one who keeps her eyes on the goal. After all, aren't all joy and peace and contentment in this life wrapped up in knowing and moving toward our Savior?

– Study/Meditation –

What does it look like to live your life right now as a marathon instead of a sprint?

Father, help me to remember that this is a life of endurance and not of "quick fixes." Forgive me when I take my eyes off of You and of Jesus. Amen.

A Teachable Attitude

Philippians 3:15

"Let those of us who are mature think this way, and if in anything you think otherwise, God will reveal that also to you."

Christian maturity requires a teachable attitude in all instances. It also requires patience and tolerance for those who are still immature in their faith, remembering that this life is indeed a process and not an instantaneous arrival.

Paul has been exhorting his readers to "press on" to the goal of Christ, remembering that none of us will actually arrive there until glory but that all of us are to run this race with endurance and focus. The applicable word here is "run" – this is a race in which we must continue to strive and work, not one where we sit back and wait on someone else to do it. Paul would never have subscribed to the "Let go and let God" theory of living.

Whereas we trust in our Father's sovereign love, we also know that "those of us who are mature" continue to strive more and more toward Jesus, as Paul said, "So that I may know him and the power of his resurrection, and may share his sufferings, becoming like him in his death." (3:10) We move steadily in our own races while patiently helping our brothers and sisters in theirs. However, we also humbly recognize that none of us has it all figured out. Instead we pray for God's wisdom and revelation in order that we truly see His way and His will in our lives.

– Study/Meditation –

In what areas of your life is God calling you to have a "teachable attitude"?

Father, help me to see the areas in my Christian walk where I need to be humbly taught in maturity. Help me to be patient with those who may be at a different spiritual place than me, keeping a gentle disposition at all times. Amen.

Holding Yourself Accountable

Philippians 3:16

"Only let us hold true to what we have attained."

It is sometimes so difficult not to hold others accountable to what we have learned. When God brings each of us to levels of maturity throughout our lives, we have to remember that God has brought each of us to those levels, and He does so in very individual and unique ways.

What Paul is reminding his readers is again about unity. He had just called all of us to move toward Christian maturity, and then he made this very significant exception-statement in the last part of verse 15, "If in anything you think otherwise, God will reveal that also to you." In essence, Paul reminding all of us that maturity is a God-inspired trait, not a you-inspired trait. We are to be patient with one another, realizing that if our brothers and sisters haven't reached certain truths from God's Word (as long as the lack of those truths aren't at the expense of the Gospel), God will bring them along in His time, not ours. Our biggest responsibility as in-sanctification-process believers is to conduct ourselves according to "what we have attained." In other words, we do, say, and act in ways that bring God glory and love and uplift our brothers and sisters. If each person in the Christian body were to pay attention to his/her own behaviors, making sure those behaviors glorified God, then I dare say that more people would see the church as a place they wanted to be rather than to avoid.

– Study/Meditation –

Read 1 Corinthians 8:1-13. What did Paul write to the Corinthian church regarding holding others accountable to what God has taught us? How might you need to mature in this area?

Father, thank You for teaching me in an individual way. Help me be patient with my fellow brothers and sisters who are learning differently than I am. Amen.

Role Models

Philippians 3:17

"Brothers, join in imitating me, and keep your eyes on those
who walk according to the example you have in us."

Paul has been using a succession of analogies in his letter to the Philippians in order to illustrate both the believer's stance as a child of God as well as her responsibilities as a one. He used the analogy of an accountant in 3:1-11 to show that the human merit we may think adds to our right standing with God must be counted as loss in comparison to the surpassing riches of what Christ did for us. In 3:12-16 he used the analogy of an athlete to demonstrate that the Christian walk is a marathon and not a sprint, stressing that it is our responsibility to press on toward the goal of Christ in this lifetime. Now, in 3:17-4:1, Paul is using the analogy of a foreigner, or an alien, to explain one of the most important reasons for behaving as children of God while we live on this earth: Christians should live as citizens of heaven, not of earth.

He begins this analogy with encouraging his readers to follow his example of living, as well as other proven men and women of God, not in self-exaltation, but in loving discipleship. It is vitally important that we have appropriate Godly role models while living here so that we might have concrete examples we can emulate. The world will offer pretty ones, but we must look far beneath the surface of their candy-coated exteriors. Our examples must be driven by God-centered beauty, a beauty that emanates His glory and His mercy. It's important that we ask ourselves often: On whom do I look as an example for living?

(continued)

Role Models – *continued*

– Study/Meditation –

Who are some of your role models? Why? What would the Apostle Paul say about the men and women to whom you look for guidance?

*Father, help me look to the right examples in this life, and
let me be the right example to whom others may look. Amen.*

The Pain of Sin

Philippians 3:18

"For many, of whom I have often told you and now tell you even with tears, walk as enemies of the cross of Christ."

Unfortunately, it is often human nature to exult in someone else's failures. Humanity tends to measure itself by the way it compares with others, finding solace when another fails, thereby making its own failures seemingly pale. It would be wonderful to say that this never happens in the church, but it does. Even when Paul was warning the Philippians about false teachers who had infiltrated their church, he did so "even with tears." It grieved Paul deeply that some had lost their way and were now spreading lies and half-truths throughout the church. He could have been indignant. He could have been angry or feel malice toward these men and women. Instead, their sin only brought him tears.

How? It's because Paul's love was for the church and his worth was found only in Christ. Truly, if each person in the church found his/her foundation not in what others thought of them or said about them but in the love and acceptance of the King of kings and Lord of lords, then more tears would be shed for those who stray than gossip or haughty glances.

Believer, never find solace in the failure of another, even as you keep vigilant watch that you, yourself, do not fail. Instead, pray for one another, for restoration and repentance, remaining sure that while you see the speck in your brother's eye, you don't neglect the log in your own. (Matthew 7:3)

(continued)

The Pain of Sin – *continued*

– Study/Meditation –

What did Jesus say about judging others in Matthew 7:1-5? How can you apply this teaching to the way you deal with rebellion in others?

Father, help me in my endeavor not to gossip or to exult in the failures of others. Help me love others as You love them. Amen.

Recognizing a False Teacher

Philippians 3:18-19

*"For many, of whom I have often told you and now tell you
even with tears, walk as enemies of the cross of Christ. Their
end is destruction, their god is their belly and they glory in
their shame, with minds set on earthly things."*

The word "redemption" can be one we are so familiar with as believers that we gloss over it as we read. However, to be redeemed, thus having received redemption, means that our rights and privileges and freedoms which we otherwise had lost were purchased for us. We have no rights to heaven or any of the blessings God gives, but in His mercy, God sent His Son, the Beloved, to come to this earth to purchase those rights for us by dying on the cross in payment for our sins. In short, we have redemption through the blood of Jesus Christ.

Paul also says in these verses that this redemption is for the forgiveness of our trespasses "according to the riches of his grace, which he lavished upon us." Probably one of the hardest things for some of us to do is to really accept, beyond a shadow of a doubt, that we have been forgiven of our sins. We look into the mirror and see all that we are, and the reality of that sinful creature can make us doubt God's forgiveness. But Paul reminds us that it was given because of God's grace, not our actions, and that grace was actually lavished on us. It was given so completely that it literally covers us with excesses of grace!

What a loving and awesome God we serve!

(continued)

Recognizing a False Teacher – *continued*

– Study/Meditation –

How have you seen the "self-esteem" movement infiltrate the church?
Why does self-esteem have no place in the Gospel of Jesus Christ?

*Father, help me to be wise and discerning when listening
to those who are teaching Your Word. Thank You for
Your Word which is a light to my path. Amen.*

Evidence of Citizenship

Philippians 3:20

"But our citizenship is in heaven, and from it
we await a Savior, the Lord Jesus Christ."

Imagine two young ladies in their early 20's. They appear to be relatively similar in appearance and ability. However, one young lady has a car, an education, a nice house, and plenty of food to eat. The other young woman lives in a one room shanty with the rest of her family, has no transportation, no education, and often goes without meals. What's the difference between these two young women? Citizenship! The first one lives in San Diego, California, and the second in a village in Uganda. If the second young woman could somehow make it to California, gain her citizenship, and move forward, her citizenship would change, and so therefore would her life. Paul is using the analogy of citizenship with the Philippians in order to illustrate that as citizens of heaven, they should live differently than citizens of the earth.

We too are to live distinctly different as aliens in this land, and we can do this because our focus is not on earthly things. Our focus is on the coming of our Lord: "We await a Savior, the Lord Jesus Christ." How sad when children of the King, co-heirs with Him to all that heaven has to give, live as paupers in a land that is not their own. Fellow Christians, live now so that the dying world might see the glory of our King and the joy of knowing that the pain of this earth is not our end. Indeed, Jesus brings our beginning.

– Study/Meditation –

What hope does God give us, His children,
about our inheritance in Ephesians 1:11-14 ?

Father, thank You that You have made me an heir with Your Son to all the
riches of heaven. You are glorious and merciful and loving. Amen.

Eagerly Waiting

Philippians 3:21

"(But our citizenship is in heaven, and from it we await a Savior, the Lord Jesus Christ), who will transform our lowly body to be like his glorious body, by the power that enables him even to subject all things to himself."

To live as the world does, as if this life on this earth is the best things will ever be, is a sad and hopeless life. That is precisely why Paul reminds us that we should live now like the citizens we are, citizens that will live eternally in heaven. What's more, we will live eternally in bodies that are glorified, without the decay and disease that exists within them now. Our bodies will "be like his (Jesus') glorious body." Not only will we be physically made new, but we will also be spiritually renewed where we will live forever with our Lord without sin and the pain it brings to everyone and everything in its wake.

How? Paul tells us that Jesus will do this "by the power that enables him even to subject all things to himself." He is God. Jesus Christ, our loving Savior, is the King of kings and the Lord of lords. Remember that Paul already wrote in 2:9-11 of this letter, "Therefore God has highly exalted him and bestowed on him the name that is above every name, so that at the name of Jesus every knee should bow, in heaven and on earth and under the earth, and every tongue confess that Jesus Christ is Lord."

Understand that when He returns, He will subject every single being to His power and reign, either willingly or unwillingly. We live now with Him as our Savior, or we perish then with Him as our Judge.

– Study/Meditation –

Why do so many not want to think of Jesus in terms of judgment? How does seeing Him as both Savior and King alleviate any misinterpretation of His power?

Father, thank You that eternity awaits me in heaven. Thank You for Your Son, Jesus Christ, who has procured for me this eternity. Amen.

The Sum of Your Life

Philippians 4:1

"Therefore, my brothers, whom I love and long for, my joy and crown, stand firm thus in the Lord, my beloved."

This first verse of Chapter 4 really ought to be included at the end of Chapter 3 since Paul begins this sentence with the word "Therefore." This word always points back to the previous points made, basically saying, "Because of this, then this." Consequently, Paul was writing that because we are citizens of heaven, knowing that Jesus will return to take us on to eternity to live with Him in glory and perfection, then we should "stand firm thus in the Lord."

This is sometimes very difficult. Things here can be so distracting and even enticing. However, we who know Christ Jesus as our Lord and Savior are "in Him," which is to share in both His righteousness and His promises. John wrote in 1 John 5:20, "And we know that the Son of God has come and has given us understanding, so that we may know him who is true; and we are in him who is true, in his Son Jesus Christ. He is the true God and eternal life." There is no other ground more firm than that of our Lord, who has already defeated death and procured eternal life for those of us who have believed on Him.

Are you struggling today with heartache from sin or circumstances? Does it seem like life is too difficult and that the weight is too heavy? Stand firm, fellow believers! This present trial is not the sum of your life; Jesus is, and He will come again to take you home.

– Study/Meditation –

Read Colossians 3:1-4. How does Paul remind us in this passage to stand firm in Christ?

Father, help me as the trials of this life seem so large that I take my eyes off of Christ and the eternity He has procured for me. Thank You for giving me this hope. Amen.

When a Christian Hurts You

Philippians 4:2-3

"I entreat Euodia and I entreat Syntyche to agree in the Lord.
Yes, I ask you also, true companion, help these women, who have
labored side by side with me in the gospel together with Clement and the
rest of my fellow workers, whose names are in the book of life."

There's an old rhyme that goes, "To dwell above with the saints we love, O that will be glory; but to dwell below with the saints we know, now that's a different story!" It's very difficult to agree with everyone all of the time and it's even more difficult to get along with them. Because we are working closely with each other in the church, disagreements and hurt feelings are inevitable, as it obviously was in Philippi.

It's interesting that the admonition here is to work through the difficulties so that we may labor in the gospel, not to decide who is right or wrong. When we are hurt by another believer or when we inadvertently hurt a fellow brother or sister in Christ, we must remember that we are not the point of anything – Jesus is! The advancement of the Gospel is! God's glory is! Therefore the only path we can take as children of God is one toward reconciliation and resolution, not so that someone gets to be right, but so that the work of the our Father continues.

We are all imperfect creatures working in a fallen world, but we are also unworthy but justified saints who will live together in glory for eternity. Don't give in to the temptation to make this about you or about any other person. Everything we do is to be done with our Father and His glory in mind. Is there someone with whom you need to reconcile today?

Read Matthew 5:21-26. What does Jesus teach in this part of the Sermon on the Mount about arguments with a brother or sister?

Father, forgive me for holding anything against one of my brothers or sisters, and forgive me of the times I have offended one of them. Help me to seek reconciliation with any in this situation. Amen.

Always Joyful?

Philippians 4:4

"Rejoice in the Lord always; again I will say, Rejoice."

Everyone wants joy. That's a pretty safe statement to make, but can anyone always have joy? Does that mean we are supposed to walk around with a perpetual smile on our faces? Is it a sin then to be depressed? Do we deny pain or sorrow? It would have made so much more sense for Paul to say, "Rejoice in the Lord some of the time" or "Rejoice in the Lord most of the time," but he says the seemingly impossible "always." How?

Understand first that this joy of which Paul speaks is a supernatural joy; it is "in the Lord." It is not a simple feeling, and it does not deny that there is pain and sorrow in this life. Jesus openly wept when He found his dear friend Lazarus dead, and much of the psalms are written by men who are expressing profoundly deep sorrow. However, to have joy in the Lord is to have joy that is not a superficial happiness based on circumstances or on the absence of trials, but rather a solid, abiding contentment and hope founded on the sure promises of God found in His Word.

Sadness and pain are a real inevitability while we live here in this time, but resting in our Father's sovereign love and grace brings an abiding peace that is manifested in the joy of which Paul speaks. Jesus said in John 16:33, "I have said these things to you, that in me you may have peace. In the world you will have tribulation. But take heart; I have overcome the world." The pain and sorrow you experience now first passed through God's love and wisdom. He will use it both for your good and His glory. In this knowledge is the joy that we can and should have "always."

– Study/Meditation –

Read David's words in Psalm 57. Where did David's thoughts go even in the midst of such despair? What does this teach you about how to respond in times of deep sadness and pain?

Father, You are gracious and good. I will praise You even in my pain. I choose to rejoice in You no matter what comes. Amen.

When is Right Wrong?

Philippians 4:5

"Let your reasonableness be known to everyone. The Lord is near."

In an age of women's rights, gay rights, consumer rights, labor rights, children's rights and every other minority group's rights, demanding our rights has become almost the definition of humanity. One of America's first flags during the American Revolution featured the motto, "Don't Tread on Me." We are prone, if not predisposed, to demand our rights, and we almost automatically do so if we feel we have been treated unfairly or spoken to unkindly or dealt with unjustly.

However, in light of his previous statements to agree in love so that we might rejoice in the Lord always, Paul now tells us to be "reasonable" with everyone. He is speaking of the fruits of the Spirit – patience, gentleness, kindness, peace, goodness – all rolled up into one character trait: forbearance. Biblical forbearance means graciously refraining from insisting on our own rights because we put love for others ahead of love for ourselves. This is directly related to our joy in the Lord.

When we are irritated by someone else's behavior toward us, then our joy is interrupted. When we respond with, "She has no right to speak to me that way!" then we have traded our peace and contented joy in God's love for what we deem as our right to be treated fairly. Paul reminds us that "The Lord is near." He is coming soon, and just as we revel in the truth that He will not treat us in "fairness" according to what we deserve, we offer the same grace and forgiveness to others, even if they have trampled on our "rights."

Read Matthew 7:12-14. What did Jesus say in the Sermon on the Mount about this principle of forbearance?

Father, please forgive me for my self-centeredness when I demand "fair treatment." Help me to patiently love my brothers and sisters in kindness and grace. Amen.

Nothing is Too Big for God

Philippians 4:6

"Do not be anxious about anything, but in everything
by prayer and supplication with thanksgiving let
your requests be made known to God."

An article in the Reader's Digest described anxiety as "a thin stream of fear trickling through the mind. If encouraged, it cuts a channel into which all other thoughts are drained." (Arthur Roche, Reader's Digest [6/88], p. 64). In truth, the word "anxiety" is the same word that Jesus used in the Parable of the Sower when He said, "And as for what fell among the thorns, they are those who hear, but as they go on their way they are choked by the cares and riches and pleasures of life, and their fruit does not mature." (Luke 8:14) That's why this verse is written in the form of a command, "Do not be anxious about anything." To do so is to display a lack of faith in God's provision.

Instead of faithless worry, Paul tells us to boldly beseech our Father in "prayer and supplication." In other words, we lay our cares and our worries at His feet, asking Him to take care of them, and then trusting that indeed He will. Often if we do so while remembering how faithful He has been, then in thankfulness our faith will be bolstered so that even in the midst of uncertainty about our finances or our health or our children or our marriages, we can know and believe Jesus when He said, "Peace I leave with you; my peace I give to you. Not as the world gives do I give to you. Let not your hearts be troubled, neither let them be afraid." (John 14:27)

A woman asked, "Should we pray about the big and the little things, or just the big things?" The answer came, "Madam, do you think there is actually anything that God considers big?"

What comfort do you receive from
passages such as Hebrews 4:14-16?

*Father, I give to you my worries and concerns, trusting that
in Your hands they are covered and taken care of. Amen.*

True Peace

Philippians 4:7

"And the peace of God, which surpasses all understanding,
will guard your hearts and your minds in Christ Jesus."

The world is full of psychological and metaphysical techniques claiming to bring one "inner peace." Repeating phrases, concentrating on one's "happy place," clearing the mind – all of these and more have been attempted so that when troubles strike, a person might find calm and tranquility. Even if these things seem to work, they will only work in the temporary and are certainly not lasting.

This is not what Paul is speaking of. As a matter of fact, Paul isn't speaking of peace that is of us at all. This peace that literally guards the core of a believer's being like a sentry standing post in war is the "peace of God." It is the peace of Jesus Christ, the very peace He told us He would leave with us in John 14:7. This peace is humanly unexplainable because it is supernatural. God's peace is not a quick fix where we say a prayer and then we receive the calm needed to get us through a crisis. This peace is everlasting, and any trouble that invades our lives must pass through it first. God's peace surpasses our understanding because it is not of us. It is of God, and He is anxious over nothing.

What an amazing God we serve in that He has bestowed on us not only His love and His grace, but His very peace stands guard over our hearts and our minds so that no matter what tragedy besets us, we may abide in Him with a contented spirit. Why? Because He promised that He has a plan for us, one that will bring us a hope and a future and will not harm us. (Jeremiah 29:11) Amen!

– Study/Meditation –

Read Jeremiah 29:11-14. What is the complete
promise of God which gives us true peace?

*Father, I give all of my troubles and trials to You, for You
are my God and my Deliverer. In You do I trust. Amen.*

My Thought Life

Philippians 4:8

"Finally, brothers, whatever is true, whatever is honorable, whatever is just, whatever is pure, whatever is lovely, whatever is commendable, if there is any excellence, if there is anything worthy of praise, think about these things."

An old Native American Christian was explaining to a missionary that the battle inside of him was like a black dog fighting a white dog. "Which dog wins?" asked the missionary. The old man answered, "The one I feed the most."

So it is with our minds. We will invariably become what we think on the most, what we feed our souls the most, and Paul rightly exhorts us to center our minds on the list of things in verse 8 after calling us to right relationship with one another and toward seeking joy and peace in the Lord. We will not have those things if we don't think on those things. Please understand that Paul is not the forerunner of Norman Vincent Peale's thoughts on "The Power of Positive Thinking." The apostle is absolutely not telling us that if we think happy thoughts that we will be happy. What he is telling us is what Jesus told us in Matthew 12:35, "The good person out of his good treasure brings forth good, and the evil person out of his evil treasure brings forth evil." Paul is not admonishing us to think "positively." He is admonishing us to think "truthfully," and truthful thinking always originates in God's Word.

If we believe that God is sovereign and full of grace and mercy, which indeed we do, then no matter what our circumstances, we must think on the things Paul lists in regards to our Father. The natural byproduct will be right relationship (V.3), joy (V. 4), peace (V.7), and contentment (V. 11).

What is the difference between what Paul says in
Philippians 4:8 and what Peale wrote in "The Power of
Positive Thinking"? (Hint: Which is focused solely on God?)

*Father, You are truth, honor, just, pure, lovely, commendable,
excellent, and worthy of all praise. I love You. Amen.*

Christian Mentors and Teachers

Philippians 4:9

"What you have learned and received and heard and seen in me – practice these things, and the God of peace will be with you."

Teachers of God's Word are so very important to the Christian life and to her sanctification. Mentors and examples and mature Christian men and women must be sought after in our lives so that we might see a model of who we are to be in Christ. But above all of that, we must look to them only as they point us to the bible. We learn and receive and hear the Words of our Father both from their mouths and in their lives so that we might grow in Him as well.

Consequently, what we glean from these godly examples is the importance of leaning on God's Word in all things so that "the God of peace" will be with us. Yes, He is always with His children, but the more we know of Him and the more time we spend with Him, the more we sense His presence. It is a special kind of communion that moves from the intellectual to the experiential.

Let us not be like the woman who told her pastor after the service, "That was an excellent message, Pastor! It was perfect for someone I know!" Instead may we look to our teachers and our mentors as avenues by which we see God's Holy Word – learning it, receiving it, and hearing it, so that we might more enjoy the intimate experience of God's peace in our lives.

– Study/Meditation –

Who in your life is a godly example? How are you working at your own sanctification so that you might also be a godly example to someone else?

Father, thank You for Your Word and for the people You have placed in my life as examples of how to follow it. Help me see the areas in my life where I need to be sanctified more so that I, too, might be a godly example to someone else. Amen.

Godly Love

Philippians 4:10

*"I rejoiced in the Lord greatly that now at length you
have revived your concern for me. You were indeed
concerned for me, but you had no opportunity."*

Although Paul is speaking most specifically here about financial support, he is also speaking of his joy that the Philippian Christians were as concerned for him as he was for them. He was far away, chained to a Roman guard twenty-four hours a day, and he had been worried for their emotional, physical, and spiritual safety. That's one of the reasons he was sending Epaphroditus to them. However, he was relieved and comforted in their love for him, which they were able to express by sending him a financial gift. Roman prisoners weren't given food and clothing like they are in American prisons. Either people they knew provided for them, or they got nothing. That made this gift all the more precious, but even that practical need was outshined by the love Paul felt from his Philippian brothers and sisters.

It is of the utmost importance that we financially support our missionary brothers and sisters all over the world, but it is also equally important that we let them know we are thinking and praying for them. A missionary's life is a lonely life. It can feel sometimes like one is all alone in his/her quest for spreading the Gospel of Jesus Christ. If you have the opportunity, send a letter or a note with your financial gifts. Much like Paul, the missionary receiving both will be comforted.

– Study/Meditation –

To whom can you tell that you are concerned for them and
care for them in the service to God's kingdom today?

*Father, show me how I can be a comfort and support to those who are on the
front lines in Your Kingdom work. Help me see every opportunity to make them
aware of my concern for them, both spiritually and practically. Amen.*

Rest for Your Soul

Philippians 4:10-11

*"I rejoiced in the Lord greatly that now at length you have revived
your concern for me. You were indeed concerned for me, but you
had no opportunity. Not that I am speaking of being in need, for
I have learned in whatever situation I am to be content."*

The definition of godly contentment is, "An inner sense of rest or peace that comes from being right with God and knowing that He is in control of all that happens to us." Notice that Paul wrote to the Philippian church that he "rejoiced in the Lord" that they were able to send him financial support. His joy at receiving the gift was not in the gift, nor was it even in the Philippians. His joy was "in the Lord." He fully rested and trusted God to supply all of his needs, so therefore when his needs were met, he rejoiced in his Father, their truest source.

Herein lay true contentment, that no matter our circumstances, we rest in the sovereign love and care of our Lord to take care of us. However, this is not an instantaneous condition. Paul said, "For I have learned in whatever situation I am to be content." This is literally a gradual transformation, one we learn by walking with God every day. As trials and tribulations beset us, God shows His faithfulness over and over so that we grow to trust Him more and more. We therefore learn to be content, because this kind of contentment is the result of the assurance we gain from living in His continual and faithful care. Paul had to learn godly contentment and so do we.

Do not fret, fellow Christian, that you may not have attained this level of peace. Walk daily with Your Father. Watch His work in your life. He will prove Himself faithful again and again, and the godly contentment you seek will come.

In what ways has God proven Himself faithful to you in the past? Why is it important that we remember those times?

Father, thank You for Your never ending faithfulness.
You are great and worthy of all my praise. Amen.

Contentment

Philippians 4:12

"I know how to be brought low and I know how to abound. In any and every circumstance, I have learned the secret of facing plenty and hunger, abundance and need."

Of course, Paul had stated this secret in verse 11 – contentment – and that contentment is in Christ Jesus. Often it is a difficult thing to reach this sometimes elusive state of mind, and that is because we have determined contentment to be found in things rather than in Jesus. We think that if we just have enough money so that we can retire or if we just have the right size of house or the right kind of job, then we will live in peace and prosperity which will consequently bring us contentment.

However, notice what two places Paul lists as those in which he had to learn to find contentment. He said that he had learned the secret "of facing plenty and hunger, abundance and need." When we don't have enough, we worry about how to get more. When we have all that we need, we worry about either losing it or still about getting more. In neither of those scenarios are we placing our peace where it should be, in our Savior.

The reality is that material things will be lost in time. Eventually either they will leave us or we will leave them, but Jesus said, "I will lose none of all that the Father has given me, but will raise them up on the last day." (John 6:39) This so-called "secret" that Paul speaks of that ends in contentment is Jesus, and He has pledged Himself to us.

– Study/Meditation –

Read 1 Timothy 6:6-11. How does Paul instruct Timothy on how to find godly contentment?

Father, thank You for never leaving or forsaking me. In You I find my rest. Amen.

No Fear

Philippians 4:13

"I can do all things through him who strengthens me."

The literal translation of this verse is, "I can do all things in Him who continually infuses me with strength." However, the question arises as to what exactly are the "all things" to which Paul is referring? Does this mean that any and all things that are available for me to do, I can do in Christ? Unfortunately, many Christians have mistakenly taken Paul's meaning to be just that, and with that interpretation come disappointment, disillusionment, and man-centered philosophy.

Paul has been admonishing us to humility, service, obedience, right relationship with one another, righteous thinking and actions, perseverance, and contentment. In short, we are to be holy and set apart as God's chosen people. These are the "all things" to which Paul is referring, things that are both of God and through Him.

Unfortunately, in our flesh we cannot do any of the things that make us a holy people, but "through Him who strengthens" us, we can. Paul is reminding us that we can do everything we are called to do in and through the power of Jesus Christ who has wholly given Himself to His children. "And God is able to make all grace abound to you, so that having all sufficiency in all things at all times, you may abound in every good work." (2 Corinthians 9:8) There is no fear in Christ; there is only grace.

– Study/Meditation –

What "all things" is God calling you to that maybe you feel inadequate to do?

*Father, thank You for giving me the grace to accomplish
all the things to which You have called me. Amen.*

Sharing One Another's Burdens

Philippians 4:14

"Yet it was kind of you to share my trouble."

Sometimes sharing our burden is the one thing that brings us comfort, right? As a matter of fact, we are a verbal people, and we are so because that's the way God created us. Adam and Eve communed with God regularly in the Garden of Eden before the Fall. They talked with Him, and He talked with them. Consequently (and this is true whether you're male or female), we work through things better when we share them with others.

Additionally, we feel better just knowing that someone else is praying for us and thinking about us in the midst of life's troubles. We want to know that we aren't alone. Paul was thanking the Philippian church for their care and concern, saying that it was "kind" of them to actually share in his trouble. What he was thanking them for was the level of love that really does feel badly when the one you love feels badly. That's the kind of love we are to have for one another in the church, and much like he has for much of this letter, Paul is calling the Philippian church to continue in unity and love for one another, demonstrated in the way they treated Paul during his trials.

The church is our family, and it will be our family for all of eternity. There is an admonition here on two sides for all of us who belong to this family: 1. Be willing to share your burdens with your brothers and sisters, and 2. Be willing to share in the burdens of your brothers and sisters. This is what family does, and honors the Father of this family.

How can you improve in both sharing your burdens with your church family as well as sharing in the burdens of your church family?

Father, thank You for giving me an eternal family.
Help me to better see how I can be a more central part of my
church, caring for them and allowing them to care for me. Amen.

82

My Treasure

Philippians 4:15-16

"And you Philippians yourselves know that in the beginning of the gospel, when I left Macedonia, no church entered into partnership with me in giving and receiving, except you only. Even in Thessalonica you sent me help for my needs once and again."

Faithful giving to the church and to the Lord's work can sometimes be a touchy subject. "This church or that ministry is always after my money," is a common complaint. The attachment we have to our pocketbooks is something that often plagues our relationships with God, and it is nothing new.

Jesus knew this and preached on it. Sixteen of His 38 parables dealt with how to handle money and possessions. In the Gospels, one out of every ten verses dealt directly with money. The bible itself offers over 500 verses on prayer, 500 verses on faith, and more than 2000 verses on money. We are preoccupied with having money, and then we are preoccupied with keeping it.

However, Paul had obviously taught the relatively new Philippian church the importance of supporting God's kingdom, so that they sent him gifts soon after he left them to spread the gospel to other places. There was no hesitation from them in sending Paul monetary support because they were assured of where their riches actually lay. This place and these things that we have now are only temporary, and they have nothing to do with our eternity. All things, including our money, are for the building up of God's everlasting kingdom. What kingdom are you building?

– Study/Meditation –

How does what Jesus taught in Matthew 6:25-34
help us with our focus on heavenly or earthly things?

*Father, forgive me for putting so much worry and time
into building up an earthly kingdom that will not last.
Help me see the places where I might instead use what
I have now to build up Your eternal kingdom. Amen.*

83

Paying it Forward

Philippians 4:17

"Not that I seek the gift, but I seek the
fruit that increases to your credit."

Many of us have investments that we have made to save for retirement or an emergency. We may invest in stocks or mutual funds or a business venture. We may be investing time and energy toward a project that promises to offer a return on our investment. However, we always go into these ventures knowing that there is some risk of losing whatever we have put into it, whether it is money or time. We also know that the higher the risk, the higher the opportunity for return and with that the higher chance for failure.

In this verse, Paul is using accounting terms, and he's telling the Philippians that the gifts they send him to support God's work are actually investments they are making into a heavenly bank account. Paul knows that God will supply whatever he needs to do the work set before him. He doesn't seek gifts from the Philippian church in order to meet his needs; he seeks them in order that their needs are met in the form of an eternal investment.

When we put our time and our money toward God's kingdom work, we are investing in a perfect and eternal return, one with absolutely no risk and a guaranteed return. It is our flesh that feels as if we are sacrificing something when we give. It is the Spirit that assures us that what we are doing is paying it forward toward a safe and eternal bank account.

– Study/Meditation –

Read Luke 16:1-9. What was Jesus teaching that
relates to Paul's point in Philippians 4:17?

Father, help me to see where I am to be generous with my
earthly wealth, paying forward into Your kingdom. Amen.

84

Giving

Philippians 4:18

"I have received full payment, and more. I am well supplied, having received from Epaphroditus the gifts you sent, a fragrant offering, a sacrifice acceptable and pleasing to God."

Paul describes the gifts sent by the Philippian church as "a fragrant offering, a sacrifice acceptable and pleasing to God." This is terminology out of the Old Testament describing the sacrificial gifts offered up to God on the altar. It is also the same terminology Jesus used to describe His sacrificial death on the cross for our sins. (Ephesians 5:2)

The point is that when we give to the church or to a ministry or to a missionary, we aren't giving to that particular person or organization; we are giving to God Himself. Suppose that Jesus Christ was the one walking down the isle of your church carrying the offering plate. When He extended that plate to you and you saw His nail-scarred hands, would you wave Him off and say, "Nothing this week"? Or would you gladly give all that you had to Him out of love and devotion to your Lord and King, thinking only of your gratitude and not your want?

We are asked to give to God's work as an act of worship unto Him, not unto any human being. If we were to keep that truth in the forefront of our minds, how much more would His work be accomplished on this earth?

– Study/Meditation –

Where might you be able to give to God's work that either you haven't given at all or haven't given all that you should?

Father, forgive me for when I hold onto earthly treasure as if it is mine. Show me where You would have me give my fragrant offering to You. Amen.

Security in God

Philippians 4:19

"And my God will supply every need of yours according to his riches in glory in Christ Jesus."

What a staggering thing that we can call the very Creator of the universe, "My God," but that is exactly what Paul does. Each of us has that privilege as well, and in that very astounding truth we also get every promise that our God has given to His children. Paul also exclaimed in Romans 8:32, "He who did not spare his own Son but gave him up for us all, how will he not also with him graciously give us all things?"

However, Paul made this statement on the heels of an exhortation on our giving by means of being generous in God's work here on earth. Paul is telling us that the fear of not having our needs met cannot be the reason we do not give to God's work, because when we give, God will supply all of our needs. It's likewise important that we understand that God will supply all of our "needs," not all of our "wants," and that He does so "according to" His riches, not "out of" them. In this we know that God will take care of us, just as Jesus so beautifully reminded us in Matthew 6:25-34, and He will do so because He is God and it is His character to do so.

In other words, according to God's character and the wondrous glory of His Son, God takes care of His children so that when they give to Him, their needs are fully met. This, brothers and sisters, is a peace and security that far in a way surpasses any anxiety we may have about giving to the work of the Lord.

Why is it so hard for us to trust that God will give us all
that we need on this earth so that we might be generous
in His work? How can we battle this needless fear?

*Father, thank You for taking care of me. Forgive me for my lack
of trust in You to take care of me and my family. I know that
You are faithful and will always supply our needs. Amen.*

How Great is Our God!

Philippians 4:20

"To our God and Father be glory forever and ever. Amen."

Truthfully, we all seek contentment. Everything we do in life is to that end, and what we know as believers is that only in God can we find it. He loves and cares for His children, supplying for us all good things and only good things that fulfill our needs. And yes, He is gracious enough to give us the desires of our hearts many times, too, but only as those desires are what are best for us. In that, He truly is our God and our Father. What Paul demonstrates in verse 20 is that a person who has really grasped these truths is a grateful person.

A Christian who lives in the beauty of knowing that the Creator God takes care of every single need, right down to the smallest one, lives also in perfect gratitude to this Father who provides for her. She knows that the world can take away many things, but it can never take away what God supplies, and in that there is wondrous thanksgiving. We, who have received all that we ever need and then eternity on top of that can do no less than sing, "How great is our God!"

– Study/Meditation –

Think today on all the ways God has
supplied your needs and give Him thanks.

*Father, You are glorious and mighty and loving and worthy of all
my praise and more. I love You! Thank You for loving me. Amen.*

No Favoritism

Philippians 4:21a

"Greet every saint in Christ Jesus."

It is clear that Christianity is largely relational, first as we relate to God and then as we relate to one another. "You shall love the Lord your God with all your heart and with all your soul and with all your mind," and "You shall love your neighbor as yourself." (Matthew 22:37, 39) Paul closes his letter with a final greeting, and we often skip or skim over verses like these. However, in them we see the importance of this relationship between believers as we strive together in God's kingdom.

Notice that Paul says, "Greet every saint." He is reminding us that every single person in the body is equally important and that our love and fellowship should extend to all. This means that we extend our greetings and relationships even outside of our "circle of friends," or the ones we tend toward on Sunday morning. He says to "greet every saint," which indicates that all of God's children hold the same station; we are all holy and set apart for His work. We have relationship with one another in brotherly love "in Christ Jesus" because in truth, only in Him is this possible. If you belong to a church for any length of time, you will be offended, but this cannot be the basis by which we relate to others in this family.

If we love our Father with everything in us, then we will also naturally love the rest of His children.

– Study/Meditation –

Read what Paul wrote in 1 Corinthians 12:12-27.
What does he teach in this first letter to the Corinthian church
that reinforces relationship with all of the body of Christ?

*Father, thank You for making me a part of Your body. Forgive me
when I exclude my brotherly love from some and give me more and
more opportunities to display this love to my church family. Amen.*

Unity

Philippians 4:21b

"The brothers who are with me greet you."

When Paul wrote this letter, he was in prison. It wasn't necessarily a great place to be, and many of the Jewish leaders who were against Paul were using his imprisonment to slander his name. Consequently, associating with him in this prison meant subjecting one's self to the same condemnation and slander, not to mention simply being there with him in the solitude of prison. And yet Paul told the Philippian church that the brothers who were with him also sent them their greetings. What a beautiful picture of Christian brotherhood, a picture that fulfills the mandate given in Galatians 6:2, "Bear one another's burdens, and so fulfill the law of Christ." The truth is that we may have our differences in the body of Christ. We may offend one another and not love like we should. However, we are to support one another, bearing one another's burdens and standing with one another when help is needed. This is our family, and this is how a family loves.

– Study/Meditation –

In what ways can you practically support
someone in your church family this week?

Father, thank You for making me a part of Your family.
Help me see the ways in which I can support
and love them in practical ways. Amen.

Sharing the Beauty of the Gospel

Philippians 4:22

"All the saints greet you, especially those of Caesar's household."

When Paul was in prison, the notoriously wicked Nero was the emperor of Rome. Nero came to be on the throne at the age of 17 after his mother poisoned her third husband, Claudius, who also happened to be her uncle. Five years later Nero had his mother killed because she had become too demanding, and he eventually also had his first wife killed so that he could marry another man's wife. He tortured his enemies, many of them Christians, by impaling them on wooden stakes and then setting them on fire in his garden, using their burning bodies as torches.

And yet, many of men who came to follow the teachings of Paul were of the Praetorian Guard and other high ranking officials within Nero's government, and it was these people who also sent greetings to their brothers and sisters in Christ in Philippi.

You may sometimes wish that you could work in a more "Christian-friendly" workplace or have the blessing of working in the Christian field rather than in a pagan environment, but remember that these are the places where some of the most beautiful testimonies have come in God's work. There is a reason we are called to be "in" the world, though not "of" it. God calls all of us to display His glory to the dying world around us, just as Paul did even while in prison.

– Study/Meditation –

Think of at least one person in your immediate circle during the day with whom you might share Christ. How might you do that today?

Father, thank You for the opportunities to shine the light of the Gospel in my life. Help me see the places where I might do that, and give me the courage at those times to speak up in Your name. Amen.

Only By Grace

Philippians 4:23

"The grace of the Lord Jesus Christ be with your spirit."

Grace. Truly this is the central theme for all of Paul's letters. It can be said that the entire book of Romans is contingent on this one aspect. Paul has been writing to his brothers and sisters in the Philippian church about many things – unity, false teaching, giving – and yet he ends his letter with a simple benediction that centers around the aspect of Jesus' gift of salvation that must be understood in order to accomplish any of the things the Apostle Paul speaks of, and that is most certainly grace.

If we don't understand the grace of Jesus Christ it will be completely impossible for us to be unified as a family in Him. After all, how can we possibly overlook the flaws of our brothers and sisters, living with them in harmony as we worship our Father unless we fully comprehend the grace of Jesus which has looked over all of ours? How can we discern the difference between God's truth and the lies of the enemy if we haven't first understood the basic tenets of our own salvation, tenets that are absolutely bound in the gift of grace? And finally, how can we release our iron grips on our purse strings and give to God what is already His unless we truly know how grace has delivered us from abject spiritual poverty?

Yes, Paul wanted to leave his readers with one last blessing, the one blessing without which they would never even be able to receive the rest of his letter. We, too, must go forward in our lives really and truly understanding grace, the grace that is greater than all our sin. Do you?

Read Romans 5. What can you glean from this great
chapter on the grace of Jesus Christ? How can this shape
the way you deal with both people and your finances?

*Father, You are merciful and full of grace. Thank You for gifting me
with that grace in Your Son and my Savior, Jesus Christ. Amen.*

lovetruthlive
WITH DEB WATERBURY

Teaching that the love of Christ
and the Truth of Scripture lead
to life-changing freedom

*"By this all people will
know that you are my
disciples, if you have
love for one another."*
– John 13:35

debwaterbury.com

lovetruthlive
WITH DEB WATERBURY

PAINTED WINDOW TRILOGY:
Painted Window, Threads and White Zephyr

Follow Elizabeth Percy's allegorical
journey into discovering the love
that transforms all of our lives –
the love of Jesus, our Bridegroom.

James on the Mount

A study of the book of James as it relates
to the Sermon on the Mount.

DAILY DEVOTIONAL SERIES:

Bible devotional studies, verse by verse.

- *Galatians* (3 month devotional)
- *Ephesians* (3 month devotional)
- *Philippians* (3 month devotional)

WOMEN'S MINISTRY STUDIES:

6 Pairs of Sandals
Yesterday's Footsteps and Today's
Women's Ministry

ADDITIONAL RESOURCES AT

www.debwaterbury.com

Dr. Deb Waterbury
also offers:
Windows of the Heart Podcast Teachings
(also available through iTunes)
and
Voices of Love Blogs

Visit us on Facebook, Twitter, Instagram,
LinkedIn, Pinterest and YouTube

Note:
*Dr. Deb Waterbury continues to expand
her resource catalogue, so please log onto
her website for the most recent additions.*

Made in the USA
Monee, IL
05 November 2020